D0889280

CHAKWAVE

The ideas expressed in this book are intended to inspire, inform, and help readers in making decisions about their health and wellness. While the author and publisher of this book have aimed to give thorough information, opinions do not replace the medical advice of your professional healthcare provider.

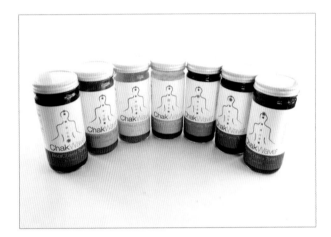

Published by Schoolyard Earth
San Francisco, California

Copyright ©2018 Jacquelyn Krieger

For ordering information or special discounts for bulk purchases, please visit www.ChakWave.com.

Cover and text design by Sheila Parr
Illustrations by Travis Brown, Steve Buccellato, and Sadie Crofts

ISBN: 978-1-7321928-0-5

First Edition

CHAKWAVE

*An Intentional Cleanse
for Body, Mind, and Spirit*

JACQUELYN KRIEGER

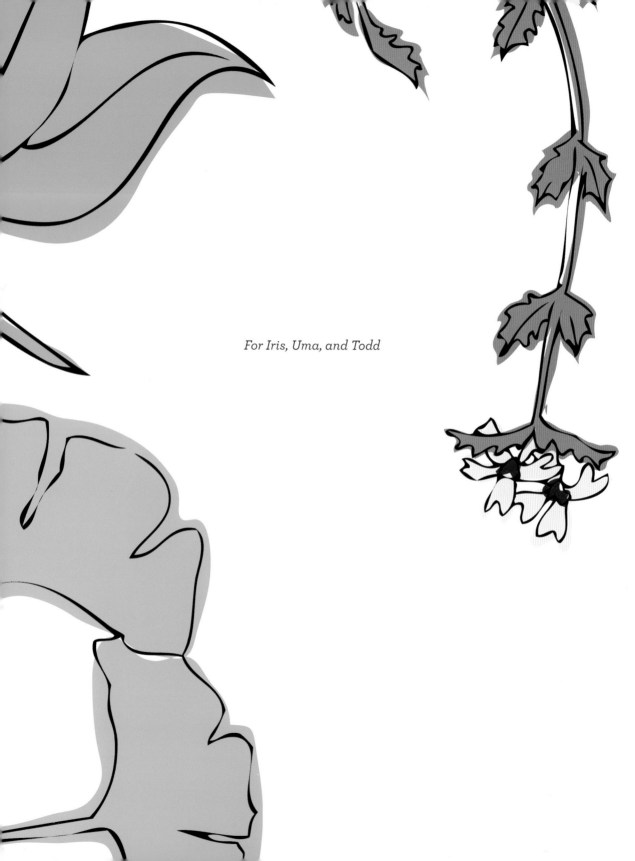

For Iris, Uma, and Todd

CONTENTS

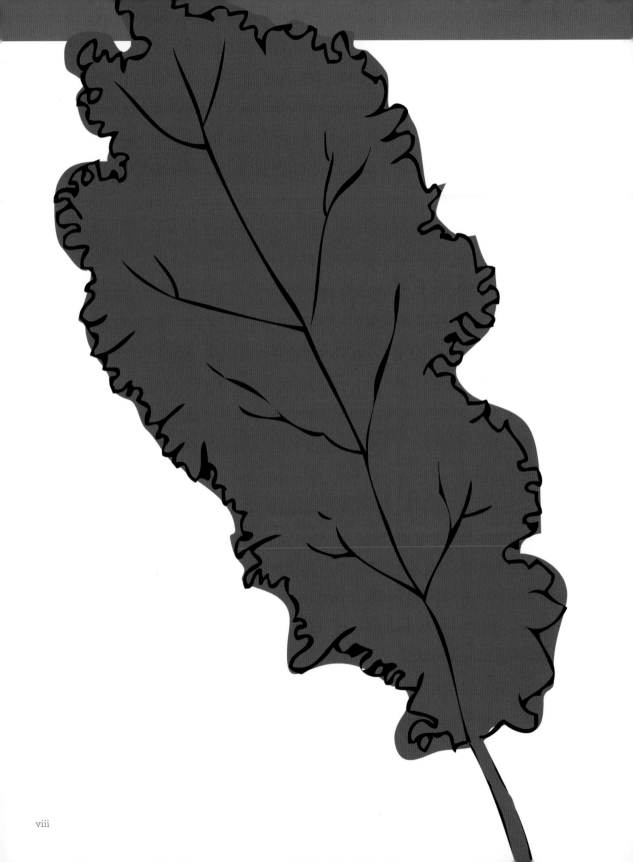

NOTE FROM THE AUTHOR

Hello and Welcome!

Thank you! Thank you for opening this book. And thank you for taking the time to take care of yourself. You have the power. In your hands. Right now. To change your life. And the lives of those around you.

Seeking to integrate body, mind, and spirit? I know I did. And so after about a decade of testing and honing this holistic system, I decided to write it down. I also wrote this to remind myself of methods for finding my center and getting back on track when I lose my way.

My intention in sharing this cleansing experience is to be of service in supporting all of us in living our fullest lives. I hope to encourage and empower you via recipes, meditations, activities, quotes, tools and tales relating to fresh juices, energy systems, health and wellness.

Let me preface this cleanse book by saying I love to eat! I enjoy food, drink, fun, and revelry. And it's also important to balance out all our joyous indulgences now and then. I've experienced profound healing when I've committed to the ChakWave cleanse, presented here as a seven day journey of physical and spiritual wellness. By creating structured space and time to cleanse, you access the potential to heal on a deep level, to lay fertile ground for a fresh start, and to sow the seeds of endless possibilities...plus maybe even an epiphany or two!

In day-to-day life, body, mind and spirit are constantly bombarded by the influences of contemporary society. We can all be affected by the world's pain, disease, destruction, and despair as well as the happiness, pleasure, love, and hope.

Taking time to cleanse helps us peel back the layers that can dim the self and prevent our inner glow from shining through.

Cleansing is a gift for yourself as well as for your family, community, and the world. Your personal commitment to raise your own consciousness can spread to those around you and bring everyone closer to a planet with more peace, truth, and forgiveness. We are like sponges that soak up both nutrients and pollutants from the air we breathe, liquids we drink, foods we eat, and environments in which we live.

The goal of this cleanse is to ingest only fresh, organic, life-enhancing elements including raw juices, herbal teas, and plenty of water while concurrently releasing physical and emotional toxins through elimination, bathing, yoga, and breathing exercises. That said, you are welcome to adjust any or all facets of the cleanse to better fit your personal desires. For those looking for a shorter cleanse or wanting to incorporate food into the week of cleansing, I have provided suggestions for modifications. Even if you don't choose to make any of the juices, you may still read the information, check out the journal prompts, and take a moment to reflect.

After hearing about the chakra system for years in yoga classes, I had an intensely moving experience in the midst of a three hour Kundalini class where I felt powerful energy swirling inside of me. It was this sudden moment within the nexus that led me on a decade-long journey seeking deeper understanding of the flow of energy. On a quest to learn how to feed and fortify these colorful energy centers, I ventured into the world of doctors, herbalists, healers, scientists, shamans, chefs, and yogis. These adventures culminated in the creation of ChakWave juices.

Juice is one of the purest forms of nourishment. I am in awe of the botanical realm and in service to the power of plants. After countless spills and thrills in kitchens plus many a bloody-beet-juice-splattered-ceiling, I landed upon what you see here, the seven ChakWave blends of vegetables, fruits, herbs, and spices inspired by each of the colorful chakras.

Within the framework of a seven day cleanse, I began sharing my homemade juices with friends, family, and other health seekers in Venice, California. Soon I was delivering the juices all over Los Angeles. Participants experienced radical change: unfulfilling jobs were left behind, relationships evolved, and minds and bodies were awakened. I also found my own passion for helping to ignite the spark in people to embrace their most honest state of being through consciousness, creativity, nutrition, meditation, herbalism, yoga, mindfulness, and energy work.

Growing up on a ranch in rural Texas, I enjoyed an early relationship with nature. Swimming in creeks and jumping on hay bales were my norm. Grounded by my earthy childhood, the discovery of yoga and chakras has been, and continues to be, a series of revelatory lessons for me. Gaining the strength to move beyond limiting beliefs, I've blown open my own heart to a place where I am constantly amazed by the vast potential of people and the planet.

It isn't always a smooth ride, but the practical chakra system helps me to live life with more presence and grace. Organizing and taking part in the ChakWave cleanse time and again has changed my life for the better. If you find this pathway inspiring, I'm hopeful it can assist you in your personal evolution as well, and perhaps we can make one more positive connection in the communal web connecting us all. I am grateful for the opportunity to share these ideas and to grow alongside you.

~Jacquelyn

Part I

INTRODUCTION

The chakras represent the architecture of the human soul.

—Anodea Judith, PhD

WHAT IS A CHAKRA?

A chakra is a vortex of constantly moving energy. Imagine subtle energies flowing and rotating like gears or becoming blocked and stagnant dependent on our physical, emotional, and spiritual wellbeing. In Sanskrit, the classical language of India, chakra literally means "wheel." While there may be thousands of chakras in a body, for simplicity's sake seven primary chakras are usually focused on. They are often depicted as spinning wheels of light forming a ladder from the base of the spine to the top of the head.

Knowledge of the chakra system was passed down orally for generations and documented in Vedic texts around 5,000 years ago, predating modern religions. Ayurveda, the Science of Life, utilizes chakras, foods, herbs, routines, rituals, meditations, elements, and environments in order to balance unevenness in the body, mind, and soul.

Chakras provide a language for the unseen. Simultaneously tangible and symbolic, the spiraling energy of the chakras corresponds with glands in the endocrine system, organs in the body, and nerve ganglia of the spinal column as well as mental, emotional, and spiritual health. Also, each chakra corresponds directly with a color of the rainbow.

TO ACHIEVE EXCELLENCE, WE MUST ALSO CONSIDER AND WORK WITH WHAT IS NOT APPARENT, WITH WHAT CANNOT BE SEEN. WE MUST JOURNEY INTO THE COMPLEX WORLD OF SUBTLE ENERGIES.

—*Cyndi Dale*

Think of your body as a prism. The white light that shines into the prism is the divine life energy that runs through you. This is often called prana, chi, qi, force, charge, shakti, subtle energy, or spirit. The chakras serve as a map of life-force throughout the body, conducting energy from the earth and heavens. Streams, rivers, clouds, and tornados all naturally create this cyclone wheel effect. As non-physical entities, chakras are not bound by Earthly laws of matter, time, and space.

Butterflies in your belly, heartache, a lump in the throat . . . these euphemisms are real feelings in the human experience, and each of these sensations take place in parts of the body where concentrated energy is being emitted. In fact, the biomagnetic field of a pumping heart or a brain deep in thought can actually be measured.

While energy orbs inside and surrounding our bodies may be a radical concept for some, most people acknowledge there are forces and factors beyond visible reality. X-rays, microwaves, radio waves, and sun rays exist even though we do not see them. If chakras aren't in your wheelhouse or comfort zone, you can still work with the system as it is a pragmatic check list for organizing life.

Humans are comprised of densely vibrating energy. Cleansing, practicing yoga, meditating, singing, chanting, acupuncture, acupressure, and participating in various forms of food and color therapy are some actions used to raise vibrational resonance and facilitate in balancing the chakra system. This in turn leads to more balanced bodies, relationships, families, communities, and creations.

CHAKRA	SANSKRIT	COLOR	GLAND	ELEMENT	SENSE	SEED SOUND	VIBRATIONAL SOUND
CROWN	SAHASRARA	VIOLET	PITUITARY	SPACE	SPIRIT	OM	NG NG
THIRD EYE	AJNA	INDIGO	PINEAL	ETHER	INTUITION	AUM	MMM NNN
THROAT	VISHUDDHA	BLUE	THYROID	VIBRATION	SOUND	HAM	EE (LONG E)
HEART	ANAHATA	GREEN	THYMUS	AIR	TOUCH	YAM	AYE (LONG A)
SOLAR PLEXUS	MANIPURA	YELLOW	PANCREAS	FIRE	SIGHT	RAM	AH (AS IN GOD)
SACRAL	SWADHISTHANA	ORANGE	GONAD	WATER	TASTE	VAM	OO (AS IN RULE)
ROOT	MULADHARA	RED	ADRENAL	EARTH	SMELL	LAM	OH (AS IN ROPE)

SCIENCE IS NOT ONLY COMPATIBLE
WITH SPIRITUALITY; IT IS A PROFOUND
SOURCE OF SPIRITUALITY. WHEN
WE RECOGNIZE OUR PLACE IN AN
IMMENSITY OF LIGHT YEARS AND IN THE
PASSAGE OF AGES, WHEN WE GRASP
THE INTRICACY, BEAUTY, AND SUBTLETY
OF LIFE, THEN THAT SOARING FEELING,
THAT SENSE OF ELATION AND HUMILITY
COMBINED, IS SURELY SPIRITUAL.

—*Carl Sagan*

WHY CLEANSE?

Gunked up and groggy? Looking to feel more vibrant and healthy? Cleansing purifies the body, preventing or repairing degeneration by eliminating wastes and toxins in tissues and organs. Taking a break from foods while drinking fresh vegetable and fruit juices plus plenty of water allows the body to recharge while still accessing nutrients.

We can look at cleansing our bodies in the same way we look at maintaining our cars. If we never check, clean, or replace clogged tubes, and continue to drive them, they often break down. Chemicals and preservatives are present in much of our modern food while our "machines" are designed to run most optimally on clean, unpolluted, unprocessed fuel from Mother Earth.

CHAKRAS ARE SPECIFIC PLACES WHERE WE CAN PUT OUR ATTENTION IN ORDER TO UNWIND ANY BLOCKS IN OUR BODIES. MY EXPERIENCE IS JUST THAT THE CHAKRAS ARE LOCATIONS IN MY SUBTLE, ENERGETIC BODY TOWARD WHICH I CAN POINT MY ATTENTION TO EXPERIENCE CONSCIOUSNESS MORE PROFOUNDLY AND WITH PURPOSE.

—Elena Brower

FUN FASTING FACTS

Many animals fast when sick so as not to expend energy digesting food but instead focus it toward healing.

Enzyme-filled and nutrient-rich juices aid in increasing energy, mental clarity, and peace of mind. The shedding of pounds alongside cellular regeneration helps to lower cholesterol and strengthen the circulatory system. Skin becomes softer and smoother. As the body becomes more alkaline and balanced, the immune system is given a powerful boost, and malignant cells may even be destroyed.

When you take time to care for yourself inside and out, senses become more attuned to aromas and flavors more potent. Perception is enhanced, not dulled by stuffing your body with food which often equals stuffing emotions down as well. You gain the capacity to access the emotional core of sickness, reprogram unhealthy energetic patterns, and discover and remove blocks preventing you from residing in a place of complete wellness.

Most people who commit to cleansing enjoy the experience, finding new energy reserves, but others may encounter some discomfort. No cause for alarm as your body is working diligently to find equilibrium while allowing itself to heal. In other circumstances you might react by trying to stop the feelings by reaching for your favorite form of self medication whether it be caffeine, alcohol, or comfort food. During your cleanse it is important to stay present with the feelings and allow yourself to dig deeply into the roots of what emerges.

Cleansing increases your sense of willpower and follow through. Many ancient cultures, great thinkers, philosophers, and writers swore by the wisdom of cleansing and fasting. This practice helps remind us of our boundless potential.

FUN FASTING FACTS
Famous fasters include Plato, Mother Teresa, Rumi, Hippocrates, Pythagoras, Thomas Jefferson, Joan of Arc, and Benjamin Franklin.

*If you want to find the
secrets of the universe,
think in terms of energy,
frequency and vibration.*

—Nikola Tesla

HOW DOES CHAKWAVE WORK?

This book contains recipes for the ChakWave juice (and life!) cleanse. Making the raw, organic juice blends promotes a healthy body, mind, and spirit. The seven ChakWave blends and colors correspond to the main chakra energy points of the body. The fruits, vegetables, herbs, and spices in each recipe symbolize characteristics and elevate mindfulness of the chakra represented.

You may have heard about eating the rainbow, taking care to create colorful plates of foods that cover all the nutritional bases. This is a simple food rule to live by. If your dinner plate consists of predominantly brown, beige, and white foods, it probably doesn't contain many important nutrients to sustain a vibrantly healthy life. We thrive when absorbing the entire spectrum of the Roy G. Biv rainbow.

INGREDIENTS

For the the ChakWave journey, the juice recipes and herbal tea blends have been created for you to drink the rainbow. Coat your insides with color, and soak up a myriad of deliciously detoxifying nutrients! Why drink all seven colors? Drum roll please!

DAY 1 / RED ROOT: Beets, strawberries, apples, dandelion root, elderberries, astragalus, and goji berries pump up the immune system, act as a blood tonic, promote the processing and elimination of toxins, strengthen bones, and fight fatigue and depression.

DAY 2 / ORANGE SACRAL: Oranges, carrots, cantaloupe, calendula flower, passion flower, cinnamon bark, cayenne pepper, and paprika reduce the risk of cancer, tone reproductive organs, help reduce blood sugar and pressure, and aide in managing diabetes.

DAY 3 / YELLOW SOLAR PLEXUS: Pineapples, turmeric root, ginger root, marshmallow root, chamomile flower, and tulsi leaf promote digestion, help prevent tumors, are an effective antioxidant and combat allergies, constipation, gallstones, and motion sickness.

DAY 4 / GREEN HEART: Kale, cucumbers, peppermint leaves, hawthorne berries, rose hips, and rosemary improve circulation and heart health, are hydrating and anti-inflammatory, provide iron, calcium and vitamins K, A, and C.

DAY 5 / BLUE THROAT: Blueberries, celery, lemon, red clover blossoms, nettles, and blue vervain flower help control high blood pressure, slow down the aging process, contain electrolytes and magnesium and combat coughs, colds, respiratory issues, and free radicals.

DAY 6 / INDIGO THIRD EYE: Blackberries, grapefruits, pomegranate, eyebright leaf, ginkgo biloba leaf, and amla berries nourish eyes, stave off strokes, aide in alertness, fight gout and arthritis, lower cholesterol and provide copper, iron, and potassium.

DAY 7 / PURPLE CROWN: Watermelon, red grapes, lavender flowers, lotus stamens, and gotu kola leaves enhance brain function, improve memory, treat headaches, hydrate, promote hair growth, and help in relieving stress.

Chia seeds (yes, this is the same chia found in the famous chia pet!) can be sprinkled into each of the juices (if desired) as they are energizing and packed with Omega-3 fatty acids. Soaking up ten times their weight in liquids, they help in filling your belly up and controlling appetite. A great source of protein and soluble fiber, Aztec Warriors took handfuls of chia before battle and even used the seeds as currency.

The ChakWave cleanse is designed to be user-friendly and delicious. Each morning, a fresh batch of juice is made for the day. The recipes make about six 8-ounce cups (48 ounces) of juice jam packed with organic fruits, vegetables, herbs, and spices. That said, if you feel like having more or less, that is A-OK. Listen to your body. You may feel like drinking every juicy drop or only a couple glasses and then sticking to water. Just be sure to keep the juices refrigerated as they are alive and perishable.

Each day of your cleanse you are provided meditations, mantras, suggested activities, yoga postures, journal prompts, and more to enrich the experience. Your body, heart, mind, and soul will thank you for committing to this seven day healthy holiday, and it just may cause positive ripple effects throughout your life.

WHY RAW AND ORGANIC?

Nature knows best. Unprocessed, unadulterated, whole foods are optimally those plucked straight from the source (vine, bush, tree, earth). Many times when foods or drinks are cooked or pasteurized at high heat, vitamins, minerals, and enzymes are destroyed. Nutrients are more accessible and readily absorbed by your body when derived from the juices of raw fruits and vegetables.

Organic foods are those grown without fertilizers or pesticides. They are safer than conventionally grown harvests as they are not doused with poisonous chemicals which inevitably harm the planet and its people. Good for your body and the land, going organic is most often more nutritious and flavorful as well. If possible, support local farms by shopping at a farmers market for your juice ingredients.

And the day came when the risk to remain tight in a bud was more painful than the risk it took to blossom.

—Anaïs Nin

MYTHOLOGY OF THE RAINBOW CONNECTION

Throughout time many cultures have expressed themselves via the rainbow. Aristotle and Seneca have pondered, hypothesized, and written on rainbows. In the Bible and Torah, Genesis says God showed Noah a rainbow as a covenant to never again destroy the earth with a great flood. Australian aborigines revered the Rainbow Serpent, which came to them during "dreamtime."

A rainbow is not an actual object that can be touched, picked up, and put on a mantle. Depending on a person's perspective and the position of the sun, a rainbow moves, shifts, dissolves, or brightens. This adds to its wondrous quality. The chakras are similarly conceptualized within us.

TRY TO BE THE RAINBOW IN SOMEONE'S CLOUD.

—*Maya Angelou*

Rainbows are not only arches of beautifully multicolored, refracted light occurring after a rain or mist but also the light rays and frequencies at work every moment to make the grass green or the sky blue. Rainbows and chakras go hand in hand. In a rainbow there are an infinite amount of colors. Our human eye usually categorizes it into the classic seven colors learned in grade school. Electromagnetic radiation is what we see.

ABORIGINALS BELIEVE IN TWO
FORMS OF TIME; TWO PARALLEL
STREAMS OF ACTIVITY. ONE IS THE
DAILY OBJECTIVE ACTIVITY, THE OTHER
IS AN INFINITE SPIRITUAL CYCLE CALLED THE
'DREAMTIME', MORE REAL THAN REALITY ITSELF.
WHATEVER HAPPENS IN THE DREAMTIME
ESTABLISHES THE VALUES, SYMBOLS,
AND LAWS OF ABORIGINAL SOCIETY.
IT WAS BELIEVED THAT SOME PEOPLE
OF UNUSUAL SPIRITUAL POWERS HAD
CONTACT WITH THE DREAMTIME.

—*Peter Weir*

In Norse mythology a burning rainbow bridge connects the world of humans to Valhalla, the realm of the gods. The Greco-Romans believed the rainbow to be the pathway Iris took as she carried messages between the gods. The colorful iris of your eye is named after this rainbow goddess. Lore has it Irish Leprechauns hide their pots of gold at the end of rainbows, and the land of Oz is "somewhere over the rainbow." Even Kermit the Frog of Muppets fame invites the lovers and dreamers to make "The Rainbow Connection."

"Red, I am healthy and strong

Orange, I feel and create

Yellow, I do and have the courage

Green, I love and I'm kind

Blue, I speak and I'm calm

Indigo, I see and imagine

Violet, I know because I'm wise and I am a rainbow

I am a rainbow"

"I am a Rainbow" lyrics from the *Wee Yogis Connect* album for kids and families. WeeYogis.com

WeeYogis

Part II

PREPARING FOR YOUR CLEANSE

SCHEDULE YOUR CLEANSE TIME

Cleansing is a commitment. There is no way around it. Your priorities, social life, and routines are asked to shift. Plan ahead for your "vacation from food" by scheduling around holidays, important dinners, or any other function that may steer you off course. Enjoy the perishable food in your fridge before juice week, mark your cleanse on the calendar, greet it with anticipation, and prepare yourself for this time of nourishment, relaxation, and recuperation. Your body and soul will be grateful.

We spend hours each day contemplating what we will eat and drink at home or in a restaurant, preparing or waiting for food, eating and cleaning up after dining. Food is a huge part of our lives! The bread-breaking rituals around mealtime bring us together with our families, friends, and tribes. Stepping away from normal routines to cleanse is a challenging but worthy commitment.

Throughout the week you will have more time on your hands than usual. Because of this, special activities are suggested to complement your cleanse. I also recommend choosing a project or goal to work on throughout the week. Perhaps it is time to read a novel (or take up a pen and start one!), to plant some herbs in the garden, or paint a picture (or a wall!). Maybe you will enjoy your extra time by diving deeply into a new meditation or restorative yoga practice.

Focusing your extra energy and attention towards positive pursuits will help you stay the course and keep your hands out of the cookie jar. Plus, at the end of the week you will have a new creation or experience under your belt.

During this seven day commitment to health and well-being, you may experience a waking meditation of sorts where you are increasingly aware of your senses and feelings. Observe sensations when procuring fruits and vegetables,

TAKE A WALK

PAINT, DRAW, CUT, GLUE, OR COLOR

CLEAN YOUR CLOSET

READ AN ENCOURAGING BOOK

PLANT VEGETABLES

ACTIVITY SUGGESTIONS

WATCH A POSITIVE FILM

MAKE LOVE . . . OOH LA LA!

WRITE A BLOG POST

LAUGH

chopping, juicing, pouring, sipping, and swallowing. From washing dishes, going to work, taking baths, exercising, driving, watching television, reading, meditating, praying, caring for children, receiving a massage, or making love, prepare to be in the proverbial "zone."

If possible, I highly recommend devoting time each morning toward meditation and a short walk even if it's just around your block or to the mailbox. Be in touch with your surroundings, soak up your neighborhood, and notice the different plants or people along your pathway. Checking in with yourself before engaging in the business of the day will set you up to be much more effective in all other realms of life.

CLEANSE MODIFICATIONS

You are invited to participate in the ChakWave cleanse any way you choose. You may drink only the ChakWave juices for the week as outlined, or perhaps you might add more chia seeds to bulk up the juices for a more full feeling. A one day cleanse with a cup of each of the seven juices is a fun and effective rainbow reset, or you may find incorporating the juices alongside light meals will better fit your goals for the weeklong commitment. Check in with yourself, and always listen to your body.

Don't beat yourself up if you choose to eat. Have a handful of raw nuts, a piece of fruit, or warm broth and then assess how you are doing. Juicing by day and enjoying a healthy meal of vegetables, fruits, salad, or soup for dinner has worked for many. If you will be adding solid foods to your cleanse, do try to keep them fresh and plant-based for optimal detoxification. Your body knows best and will tell you what is working and what may benefit from some finessing.

If now is not the time to take on the seven day cleansing journey or you only have a limited amount of days to juice,

HOW OFTEN To CLEANSE?

Depends on the person. Maybe this is a once a year event (New Year Resolution!) or at the beginning of each changing season or weekend cleanses sprinkled about your year.

Buddha's Diet by Tara Cottrell and Dan Zigmond recommends eating mindfully each day within a nine hour period of time, essentially fasting for 15 hours daily. This helps insulin maintain a healthy level as opposed to spiking throughout the day, which may result in weight gain or serious chronic conditions including diabetes. www.buddhasdiet.com

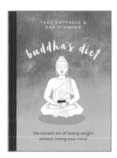

then any scenario "counts." No sweat if you don't do the entire cleanse up the chakra system. Have two days and want to focus on Root and Third Eye chakras? Then just juice those recipes and read up on the properties of each.

More of a four-day juice faster? Create your own "Cover Your Bases" cleanse from Root to Heart to address the lower chakras and establish a strong foundation. Sometimes we just need a tune up or are taking sweet baby steps toward our cleansing goals. You and only you know best what you require. Having done the cleanse a number of times throughout the years, I usually opt to drink water, sip herbal tea, and only have one or two juices per day. If you feel like juicing from the Crown down, then by all means call in that manifestation energy and ground it with Root on the seventh day. This is your adventure to choose and create!

If you do not live in a place with a bounty of fresh produce or farmers markets, remember there are no hard and fast rules in life or with juice recipes so feel free to explore combinations of fruits and vegetables and find what works for you according to taste preference, seasonality, and availability. If pomegranates aren't an option, carry on with the rest of the recipe or add a few more blackberries. If cantaloupes aren't your thing, increase the amount of carrots and oranges.

If you choose not to incorporate the herbal teas, the juices alone are delicious. Don't feel like fruit? Then make all vegetable juice. The colors may not look exactly like what you find in the crayon box, but that isn't a deal breaker. Green juice your favorite? Make the Heart recipe every day and maybe a cup of the other colors to bring in the full color spectrum. Above all, it is the intention you set that is most important.

If you are taking special medications or have any questions or concerns about cleansing, do not hesitate to consult with your health care provider/s. Reach out for support when embarking upon a new experience, and always trust your intuition. You probably would not have picked up this book unless you were interested in and ready for this healing journey.

CLEANSE WITH COMMUNITY

There is strength in numbers! Connect with other ChakWave juice cleansers online, grab a cleanse buddy or form a group, and begin your healing journey. If the going gets tough, being able to pick up the phone and break it down with your friend whom is also deep in the juiciness provides a powerful connection.

Further the buddy system by purchasing bulk produce from the farmers market and experimenting with juicing techniques with a friend. Cheer each other on; lend support and a loving ear. Connect on the meditations, journal prompts, and activities while allowing your culinary creations to permeate your organs and nourish your soul.

CHAKWAVE CONNECTS
ChakWave.com
facebook.com/chakwave
instagram.com/chakwave
#ChakWave

Understanding our health through our chakras enables us to move beyond ensuring that the body has physical food for energy to live by taking us into the realm of food as "spiritual sustenance" or "food for the soul."

— Dr. Deanna Minich

CHAKRALYN

In the midst of serious cleansing work, it can be nice to keep things light and have a laugh. This is a character that emerged for me many moons ago. I was given "Chakralyn" as my "playa name" at the Burning Man arts festival and later, was invited to bring her to cartoon life in a "Lady Yoga" comic strip in *LA Yoga* Magazine. She fights enemies of fatigue and stress by mixing up her magical chakra tonics kept in her elixir belt, and she is here now to cheer you on!

EQUIPMENT

In order to embark upon the ChakWave adventure, you will need a juicer (although some have actually made all the recipes using a blender for more of a smoothie experience). If you already have one, wonderful! If not, this doesn't have to be a wallet draining experience. Borrow one from a friend or find a "previously loved" juicer on Craigslist.

If you are in the market to purchase a perfect-for-you appliance, there are many different types of juicers out there and of course plenty of opinions from friends, family, and the web. Realistically take into consideration your available time, space, and budget. Centrifugal, with or without pulp ejection, masticating, single or twin gear juicers? Try not to get bogged down by the choices. The fact you are juicing at all is beautiful and powerful!

JUICER REVIEW

Breville, Champion, Hurom, and Omega are trusted brands in the realm of home juicing, and the Vitamix, NutriBullet, and Ninja blenders have all been used to create the ChakWave recipes as well.

For an in-depth and user-friendly analysis of juicing machines, check out Kris Carr's Ultimate CrazySexy Juicer Review: KrisCarr.com/blog/best-juicer-buying-guide

JUICE RECEPTACLES

You may like to experiment drinking your juices from a variety of containers. I prefer clear glass because I want to clearly see the vibrant juice colors! When finished slurping down the last yummy drops, glass can be easily cleaned and reused. There's no leaching of plastics or landfill waste.

The recipes make around 36 to 48 ounces of juice per day. This varies a bit depending on the produce and juicer you are working with. Lidded glass jars are pleasant to sip from, easily portable, and come in an array of sizes. Plus, I think they feel very wholesome . . . as if your Granny whipped up an herbal chakra elixir for you! No need to purchase any new containers. Use ones that best fit you and your lifestyle.

THREE DAYS BEFORE YOUR CLEANSE

For an optimal cleanse, it is wise to remove animal products from your diet at least three days before you begin juicing. Many health issues (obesity, cancer, heart disease, strokes, clogged arteries, contamination) today are exacerbated by eating animals and the products created by them. A plant-based diet causes the least amount of harm to your body as well as the world for no forests are cleared to raise animals, and no animals are caged or killed to fill a plate. Perhaps you will find during this break from normal eating patterns an opportunity to analyze and revise your own habits and traditions, a blank slate from which to start anew.

You don't have to become a breatharian! Cultivate awareness of what you're putting into your body and where it's coming from because that whole "you are what you eat" thing happens to be true.

Reduce or cut out caffeine. While a cup of joe, espresso, cola, or energy drink can be a nice treat with a quick boost, try

EAT FOOD.
NOT TOO MUCH.
MOSTLY PLANTS.

— *Michael Pollan*

not to overdo it. If you experience withdrawal symptoms like headaches, irritability, or it feels like you have the flu, remember the detox process takes time and you can get over this health hurdle.

If your attachment to caffeine runs deeply and now is not the time to release it completely, that's okay. Try mixing caffeinated teas into your regimen for a gentler change of pace or drink a reduced amount of coffee black (1 cup, not 5). Reach for purified water to energize, and grab a handful of seeds, nuts, or berries for a quick and nutritious pick me up.

Ditch alcohol. It doesn't have to be forever, but do enter cleanse mode with a clear head and hydrated body. If moments during this three day pre-cleanse or week of juicing feel emotionally unbearable and all you want to do is pour a boozy glass, notice this desire along with any feelings that crop up for you. Really feel and listen rather than going for a numbing potion. Cheerful champagne toasts and warming wine can be a lovely time, and knowing you are choosing them rather than needing them is invaluable.

During a cleanse, emotions may be intensified because you are no longer masking or medicating them as they emerge. Try not to be afraid of feeling your emotions. Negative feelings often get stigmatized in our society, but they usually come up for a reason. What if they are trying to point out issues in our lives that need attention?

Take this opportunity to get in touch with the root sources of everything you feel. Ask yourself why you hurt, explore your aches and pains, speak with a friend or therapist, take a long bath, go for a walk, or let out a quality cry. When our bodies—and lives—are out of balance, illness develops. Your body communicates in a language beyond words. The cleansing period is your opportunity to listen and heal the dis-ease.

Our business is
to wake up.

—Aldous Huxley

SAMPLE PRE-CLEANSE MENU

Enjoy a menu of fresh, organic, whole foods for three days leading up to your juice cleanse. If you stray, it's okay. Find your way back. Here is a sample menu to inspire.

Day 1
Breakfast: oatmeal with dates and cashews
Snack: vanilla chia pudding with sliced plums
Lunch: spinach salad with dried cranberries, walnuts, and apple cider dressing
Dinner: zucchini, pepper, and cilantro veggie fajitas with corn tortillas, guacamole, and salsa

Day 2
Breakfast: almond milk yogurt with granola and blueberries
Snack: hummus and pita bread
Lunch: quinoa, mango, and black bean salad
Dinner: marinated portobello mushroom steak, mashed potatoes, and wilted chard
Dessert: strawberries and coconut cream

Day 3
Breakfast: banana, avocado, and cacao smoothie
Lunch: grilled eggplant, tomato, and onion sandwich with steamed asparagus
Dinner: seaweed and tofu miso soup with edamame and veggie spring rolls

SOME GREAT PLANT BASED COOKBOOKS TO CREATE HEALTHY MASTERPIECES FROM:

Chloe's Kitchen by Chloe Coscarelli

Color Me Vegan by Colleen Patrick-Goudreau

The Inspired Vegan: Seasonal Ingredients, Creative Recipes, Mouthwatering Menus by Bryant Terry

The Kind Diet: A Simple Guide to Feeling Great, Losing Weight, and Saving the Planet by Alicia Silverstone

The Millennium Cookbook: Extraordinary Vegetarian Cuisine by Eric Tucker

The Oh She Glows Cookbook by Angela Liddon

Roberto's New Vegan Cooking: 125 Easy, Delicious, Real Food Recipes by Roberto Martin

Thug Kitchen: The Official Cookbook by Thug Kitchen

VB6: Eat Vegan Before 6:00 to Lose Weight and Restore Your Health . . . for Good by Mark Bittman

Veganomicon by Isa Chandra Moskowitz and Terry Hope Romero

ELIMINATION

Urination, defecation, perspiration, and respiration are the four avenues of elimination you are working with and encouraging this week (and always!). Keep fluids flowing in the form of juice, water, and tea for steady urination throughout the day. When your inside is moisturized, the outside becomes moisturized as well, which is visibly noticeable through a reduction in wrinkles, bloating, and puffiness.

Drink teas that aid in bowel movements. Senna or aloe vera leaf tea, licorice root, and buckthorn bark are good choices. You may want to experiment with ingesting a tablespoon of castor oil to help "slick down" your interior. Slippery insides are good as this helps everything to move freely and diffuses built up muck. Don't go overboard with these laxatives though; drink a slow and steady one or two cups of tea a day.

Abstain from wearing antiperspirant deodorant in order to allow your body to sweat out toxins. Your normal body aroma probably isn't "gross" like some advertisements may have you believe. Give it a shot when you are hanging around your home and notice your own natural smell. Hit up the steam and sauna rooms to really open up the pore floodgates! And if you must wear something, consider a dab of essential oil or a more natural deodorant. This could be a good time to go through your body products (lotions, shampoos, creams, cleansers) looking closely at the ingredients. Skin is our largest organ and absorbs all we put on it. If you wouldn't eat it, you may not want to wear it.

Follow your breath throughout the day, consciously breathing in health and wellness while exhaling the old and ill. With every oxygenating breath, focus on simultaneously calming and energizing your system. If tense, practice ujayi

AN EDUCATED PATIENT IS EMPOWERED; THUS, MORE LIKELY TO BECOME HEALTHY.

—*Dr. Dean Ornish*

breathing—inhaling and exhaling through the nose with the throat closed slightly so that you create the sound of the ocean in your throat.

DEEP CLEANSING RITUALS

Enjoy private tea ceremonies for one. The ChakWave herbal blends are potent potions to steep each morning, allow to cool, and add to the freshly prepared juices according to the recipes. Throughout your cleanse, continue adding hot water to the tea, bask in the steam, and savor the flavors. If you don't have all the suggested herbs, use one or two listed, your own choice of tea, or order pre-made packets online from ChakWave.com. Just holding a warm cup of herbal goodness can brighten your mood.

Drink up. Hydration is key. Feelings of fatigue are often signs of dehydration. A nice rule of thumb is to drink half your weight in water ounces per day. For example, if you weigh 140 pounds, that's 70 ounces. (8.75 cups). Increase by a cup for every acidic beverage consumed such as coffee, cola, or alcohol.

Squeeze fresh lemon juice into water and tea for its powerful alkalizing and cleansing effects. Lemons clean the blood and aid in regulating indigestion and constipation. Try muddling fresh herbs like mint, rosemary, lemon balm, or fennel seeds into your water as well.

Use a neti pot. A part of Ayurvedic tradition for thousands of years, this method of flushing out your sinuses with salt water is extremely effective. Allergies, congestion, and general crud run for the hills when "irrigating" your nostrils and septum. Tilt your head and tip your cute little genie pot into one nostril. Hold it steady, and stay the course as the water flows out your other nostril. At first this can feel very foreign, but soon it becomes a pleasurable experience. Do this in the shower, over the sink, or outside, and then gently blow your rejuvenated nose!

Try a morning saltwater flush. Drink a liter of warm, filtered water mixed with two teaspoons of sea salt to kick off the day. Stay near a bathroom as the effects kick in.

Pamper yourself with a moisturizing oil or lotion massage. This will invigorate the lymphatic system and help your body release toxins. Plus, it feels great.

Steam it out! If you have access to a steam room, this is the perfect time to enjoy a splendid shvitz. Sweating out the goo is one of the most immediately gratifying as well as time honored traditions for detoxifying and relaxing.

Facials are fantastic. Opt for extractions and try a mud mask to slough off old layers leaving behind a bright complexion.

Mineral-rich salt baths are extremely therapeutic. Salt water relieves stress, relaxes muscles and joints, reduces inflammation, increases circulation, and hydrates skin. Bathing salts can be found at grocery, drug, or health stores and come in an array of types including Epsom, Bokek, or Himalayan Pink to name a few. Drops of lavender, peppermint, or eucalyptus essential oils bring aroma and herbal therapy into your restorative bath time.

If you have ever considered colon hydrotherapy, a cleanse presents a perfect time to take the plunge. The process can certainly challenge comfort levels as it operates in delicate areas, but many swear by it as an age old way to flush out accumulated waste. A small tube inserted into the rectum carries fresh water in while moving waste out through a gently pressurized system. If you opt to try it, make sure to find a highly recommended and well trained practitioner.

Surround yourself with singing bowls, tuning forks, chanting, or any instruments or pieces of music that move you. From didgeridoos to banjos, music contributes to vibrational healing which can be a potent way to tune and balance the energetic body. Music is an international and inter-dimensional way of communicating with your self, others, and other ways of being. Allow your nervous system and endocrine glands to be bathed with music and calibrated to a more radiant state.

Practice pranayama—the regulation of breath through certain techniques and exercises. Nadi Sodhana, alternate nostril breathing, uses your fingers to close and open the airflow in a methodical manner. Later in the day, mix things up with Breath of Fire breaks inhaling and exhaling rapidly from the nostrils.

Tongue time! Scrape off excess build-up on your tongue with an official tongue scraper or the edge of a spoon. Best to remove all residue from your body during your cleanse, plus your taste buds will be titillated and ready for delicious, juicy action.

FASTING IS THE GREATEST REMEDY, THE PHYSICIAN WITHIN.

—Philippus Paracelsus, M.D.

Dry brush for a rush. From your feet to your arms, belly to back, brush your way towards your heart for exfoliated skin and an invigorated lymphatic system. Try kicking off the day with this energizing boost.

For an ultimate grounding experience, hop in a bathtub and from the neck down get packed in mud! In healing spas where there is access to spring waters mixed with volcanic ash, practitioners cover you up and invite you to be seriously still. Great for detoxifying the body and calming the mind.

Take a social media break. Sometimes we need to unplug. Our phones, computers, pads, tablets, apps, high-tech watches, and any other gadget that lights up or tempts us to post, scroll, or hashtag will still be there when we are done centering and experiencing low-tech peace and quiet.

Sleep. Give yourself permission for some extra between-the-sheets R&R. Rest and relaxation are incredibly healing, helping tension and stress melt away.

Ingredient list for the seven day ChakWave juice cleanse:

- 8 medium beets
- 3 cups strawberries
- 5 apples
- 1 cantaloupe
- 3 oranges
- 12 carrots
- 1 teaspoon paprika powder
- 1 teaspoon cayenne pepper powder
- 1 teaspoon cinnamon powder
- 3 pineapples (about 9 cups chopped pineapple)
- 6 inches fresh ginger (about 6 tablespoons)
- 3 inches fresh turmeric (or 3 teaspoons powdered turmeric)
- 10 cucumbers
- 15 leaves kale (2 bundles)
- 1 bundle fresh peppermint
- 4 cups blueberries
- 2 bunches of celery stalks (about 20 ribs)
- 1 lemon
- 3 pomegranates
- 2 heaping cups blackberries (about 1 pint)
- 3 grapefruits
- 1 personal sized watermelon
- 2 cups red grapes
- about ¼ cup chia seeds

CHAKWAVE ONE DAY JUICE CLEANSE

Enjoy a glass of each color of the rainbow!

ROOT: 2 large beets, 1 apple, ½ cup strawberries

SACRAL: 1 orange, 3 carrots, ¼ cantaloupe, sprinkle paprika, cayenne, and cinnamon to taste

SOLAR PLEXUS: ½ pineapple (1 ½ cups), 1 inch fresh ginger (or more if you like spice!), ½ inch fresh turmeric (or sprinkle generously with powdered turmeric)

HEART: 2 cucumbers, 3 large kale leaves (about 1 cup dark greens), sprig of fresh peppermint

THROAT: 1 cup blueberries, 4 stalks celery, squeeze of lemon

THIRD EYE: 1 pomegranate (around 1 cup seeds), ½ heaping cup blackberries, 1 grapefruit

CROWN: ¼ of a personal sized watermelon, ½ cup red grapes

CHAKWAVE HERBAL BLENDS

If you plan on drinking the teas during your cleanse, most of the herbs can be found at a local herbal apothecary or online from a company such as Mountain Rose Herbs (*www.MountainRoseHerbs.com*). They can also be purchased online pre-blended from ChakWave (*www.ChakWave.com*).

ROOT: dandelion root, elderberries, astragalus, goji berries

SACRAL: calendula flower, passion flower, cinnamon bark

SOLAR PLEXUS: marshmallow root, chamomile flower, tulsi leaf

HEART: hawthorne berries, rose hips, rosemary

THROAT: nettles, red clover blossoms, blue vervain flower

THIRD EYE: eyebright leaf, ginkgo biloba leaf, amla berries

CROWN: lavender flowers, lotus stamens, gotu kola leaf

Part III

TERM DESCRIPTIONS AND CLEANSE COMPANION

I found I could say things with color and shapes that I couldn't say any other way—things I had no words for.

—Georgia O'Keeffe

Each of the seven cleanse chapters includes a detailed description of the chakra it is inspired by along with an array of other associations from senses to sounds, mantras to meditations. The terms and practices mentioned are as follows:

SANSKRIT NAMES

Sanskrit is a language of India believed to be elevated, purified, and polished and to be used when speaking of the philosophical and sacred. Intentionally pronouncing each word can be a ritual in and of itself. To the right are the Sanskrit symbols of the chakras.

MANTRAS

Mantras are sound vibrations which help one attune to the Universe by using repetition, frequency, and pitch in order to clear and calm the monkey mind. Via rhythms and breathwork we can tap into the subconscious. Be it a subtle breeze blowing, a Sanskrit chant, Gospel hymn, folk song, or lullaby, these sounds help us silence the chatter so we may be present and aware.

COLORS

Color affects us. Consciously and subconsciously we are changed by the green of nature, the fuchsia of a sunset, the blue of the ocean. The clothing we choose to wear, the hues we paint on our wall; all of the colors we decorate our lives with have significance. Picking colors to surround yourself with is not superficial for you are summoning those wavelengths, characteristics, and energies into your life. The colors of the rainbow are in order of the wavelengths they emit, red being the longest and violet the shortest. Metaphorically, the colors represent traits and qualities in our daily lives.

Red is earthy and filled with life force. Images of fluids such as erupting lava and flowing blood are evoked. Orange combines red and yellow, which brings out creative

Vitamin C . . . Color!

characteristics of both in the form of curiosity and playfulness. Yellow powers up our bodies and minds helping us to focus, digest, and shed light on issues that arise. Green is natural, flourishing, balancing, expanding, and growth oriented. Blue is the shade of communication and expression with all the potential expansiveness of the ocean and sky. Indigo invites us to daydream, to use our perceptive abilities and imaginations expanding into the unseen. Violet is vast, light and aware, eliciting feelings of meditative peacefulness.

Each day of the ChakWave cleanse, consciously surround yourself with the color of the chakra represented. Bust out wardrobe pieces lurking in the back of your closet and don that vibrant indigo! If possible, choose clothing that is natural and breathable. Arrange bright bouquets invigorating your senses. Use a rainbow of linens, towels, yoga mats. Splish splash, take a colorful bath! Powders in an array of healing hues are sold in health stores to make your bubble bath bright. Break out the crayons or paints and get creative as you envelop yourself in curative shades.

LOCATIONS

While it is difficult to pinpoint an exact "chakra spot" in the body, the chakras are envisioned as spiraling globes lined up along the spinal cord. Located more toward the back body, they are consistent with endocrine glands and nerve ganglia in the physical form.

EVERYTHING THE POWER OF THE
WORLD DOES IS DONE IN A CIRCLE.
THE SKY IS ROUND, AND I HAVE
HEARD THAT THE EARTH IS ROUND
LIKE A BALL, AND SO ARE ALL THE
STARS. THE WIND, IN ITS GREATEST
POWER, WHIRLS. BIRDS MAKE THEIR
NESTS IN CIRCLES, FOR THEIRS IS
THE SAME RELIGION AS OURS. THE
SUN COMES FORTH AND GOES
DOWN AGAIN IN A CIRCLE. THE
MOON DOES THE SAME, AND BOTH
ARE ROUND. EVEN THE SEASONS
FORM A GREAT CIRCLE IN THEIR
CHANGING, AND ALWAYS COME·
BACK AGAIN TO WHERE THEY WERE.
THE LIFE OF A MAN IS A CIRCLE
FROM CHILDHOOD TO CHILDHOOD,
AND SO IT IS IN EVERYTHING
WHERE POWER MOVES.

— *Black Elk*

ELEMENTS

Earth, Water, Fire, Air, Vibration, Ether, and Space correspond with the chakras in order of the most condensed and sensory Root (Earth) to the most free form and extra-sensory Crown (Space). Ancient civilizations and cultures have used elements symbolically in astrology, tarot, medicine, and shamanism to exemplify the metamorphosis of all things.

SENSES

Our senses provide perceptions for processing stimuli. Our nervous system receptors detect and assimilate data giving us more information about our surroundings and experiences. Body and soul feel pleasure and pain via our sophisticated sensory gathering mechanisms. Smell, Taste, Sight, Touch, Sound, Intuition, and Spirit coincide with the chakras.

AREAS OF BODY INFLUENCED

Although not fixed rigidly within any particular location within the body, the chakras do correlate with general areas. When practicing chakra meditations or healings, it is oftentimes useful to visualize the chakras and their effect in these areas such as sending red, root chakra energy down into the feet or feeling green light rush outward from the heart through the hands as an exercise in allowing oneself to fully love.

DESCRIPTIONS

The basic properties of each chakra are laid out, energetically and how that translates to our "brick and mortar" life.

NOTHING EVER GOES AWAY UNTIL IT TEACHES US WHAT WE NEED TO KNOW.

— *Pema Chödrön*

MEDITATIONS

Meditations work well when used repeatedly throughout each day of your cleanse (and anytime you feel like a refreshing pick-me-up!) as they state, affirm, and integrate intentions with reality.

LESSONS FOR SPIRIT

Each chakra connects to attributes of existence worthy of reflection. Pondering these positive characteristics in regards to your own state of being can be beneficial towards bringing them to the forefront of your life.

UNBALANCED

Each chakra has shadow traits which can appear when balance is off kilter. Don't go to the "OMG, I suffer from every one of these so I must be broken beyond repair!" place of despair. Think of this section as a health check-up list for honest self-appraisal. These conditions may be ever changing. Once one is addressed, another can turn up wanting to be healed. The inevitable ebb and flow of life occurs.

How wonderful it is that nobody need wait a single moment before starting to improve the world.

—Anne Frank

BALANCING ACTIVITIES

Hands-on suggestions for immediate things to do, these suggested activities will help you get in touch with the characteristics of the chakra and into a mindful flow throughout the day. Complete concrete tasks while remembering your own divinity.

BEFORE ENLIGHTENMENT . . .
CHOP WOOD, CARRY WATER.
AFTER ENLIGHTENMENT . . .
CHOP WOOD, CARRY WATER.

—*Zen proverb*

VIBRATIONAL SOUNDS

By making these sounds you can actually feel the vibrations in your physical body where the chakras are located. As the sounds emanate, know you are an amazing instrument! Plow through any resistance by pitching and playing the tune only you can.

OH (AS IN ROPE)
OO (AS IN RULE)
AH (AS IN GOD)
AYE (LONG A)
EE (LONG E)
MMMNNN
NGNG (YING YING)

SEED SOUNDS

LAM, VAM, RAM, YAM, HAM, **AUM,** and **OM** are Sanskrit bija mantras. When chanting, singing, or pronouncing them, they activate, balance, and tune into the frequency of the chakras.

TONAL KEYS

Doe, a deer, a female deer . . . Ray, a drop of golden sun . . . The sounds of music bring the energy centers alive! Isaac Newton recognized and aligned the seven rainbow colors with the seven musical scale notes: **C D E F G A B.** These are the tones that resonate with the chakras, and when singing them one can feel the vibration in your body where the individual chakras lie.

GEMS, CRYSTALS, AND MINERALS

Gemstones, crystals, and minerals are not only pretty; they can aid in balancing, clearing, and revitalizing. They (like everything else) are made of energy, and their pure geometric patterns have been used in many cultures by those seeking healing and harmony. Ion-generating and containing electrical properties, crystals at work in the world include quartz clocks and titanium-sapphire tunable lasers used in particle accelerators. Notice what stones or jewelry you are intuitively attracted to . . . and rock on!

ESSENTIAL OILS

The grounding sense of smell is powerful for immersing us in the moment. Holistically healing, aromas bring awareness to the present and aide in concentration. They remind us of people, places, and evoke emotions. Whether you use oils, candles, or body washes, notice the qualities that are brought into focus. Some are calming, others invigorating. Some you may crave; others may cause you to cringe. Have fun being the alchemist in your own aromatherapy lab, inhaling and dabbing yourself with delightful fragrances.

And those who were seen dancing were thought to be insane by those who could not hear the music.

—Friedrich Nietzsche

YOGA POSTURES

The practice of yoga has provided vital nourishment to the mind, body and spirit for ages. It is art and science melded, a marriage of bodily mechanics, the elixir of breath, patience, persistence and flow. Yoga champions being present in your body, listening to desire, pushing boundaries, and knowing when to sit back and relax. Many believe yoga is a training program for living and dying with grace. In fact we "play dead" at the end of each yoga class as we melt into Savasana—Corpse Pose.

For each day of cleansing, there are suggested yoga postures relating to the chakras. Think of yoga as a microcosm of your life. Focus on being flexible in mind as well as body. Be gentle with yourself, and thank yourself for taking the time to practice. Bend and explore. Where are you rigid, intolerant, or inflexible? Flex your heart, your love, and your truth. Namaste.

"NAMASTE" is the salutation used which means "I bow to you." The gesture of placing hands at the heart and nodding the head symbolizes recognizing the divine spark in oneself and another. It is a way to show respect, gratitude, and connection to all.

BLESSED ARE THE FLEXIBLE FOR THEY SHALL NOT BE BENT OUT OF SHAPE.

—*Anonymous*

CHAKWAVE HERBAL BLENDS

The seven ChakWave blends of healing herbs, flowers, roots, and leaves correspond with the energetic chakras as well as the physical body where the chakras align. For example, the Root ChakWave tea ingredients dandelion root, astragalus, elderberries, and goji berries help in grounding and building the immune system while the Crown ChakWave tea ingredients of lavender flowers, lotus stamens, and gotu kola focus on circulation and brain health.

Of course there is some overlap of the healing properties of the herbs in each of the seven mixtures, but for the most part the focus of each tea is on the organs in the body where the chakra resides. Healing teas are a way for humans to soak up natural earth elements.

The way of tea is medicinal and harmonious. It brings nature to society connecting us to the weather and elements. The Mandarin translation describing tea preparation is "free time" for it is time to meditate and contemplate. Without rushing, take the time to steep tea as a ritual. Perfect yourself to perfect your brew, and master the self to master the brew.

Create an herbal infusion by placing a heaping tablespoon of mixed herbs in a teapot or mug. Pour half a cup of boiling water over them to ignite your aromatic masterpiece. Cover with a lid or plate and let your potent tea steep for 15 minutes. Strain, allow to cool completely, and add to your juice creations for the herbal punch. You may then add hot water to the same herbs throughout the day to enjoy multiple cups of soothing tea.

If you don't have access to these particular teas or opt to make the ChakWave recipes sans herbs, it's all good. The vegetable and fruit juice combinations stand alone. Your cleanse is still on!

Elements of a Cup of Tea

NUTRITION

Biological, historical, mythological, folkloric, and energetic information on the ingredients in each recipe is provided along with illustrations of these potent natural medicines.

JOURNALING

The journaling prompts provided at the end of each chapter invite you to put pen to paper expressing where you're at and how you're feeling. Writing your thoughts is helpful for processing emotions, healing hurts, celebrating victories, and making game plans. Let your writing be a meditation, and look for themes and guidance that may emerge. Are there any thoughts, experiences, or questions that arise for you? Scribble and color outside of the lines!

DAILY CHAKRA CHECK-IN

Ask yourself the following questions at the end of each day:

Did I meditate?

Did I engage and ignite my imagination?

Did I speak my truth and communicate effectively?

Did I love deeply?

Did I stand up for myself and stay focused on my goals?

Did I play and use my creativity?

Did I keep my space clean and organized?

Part IV

CLEANSE TIME

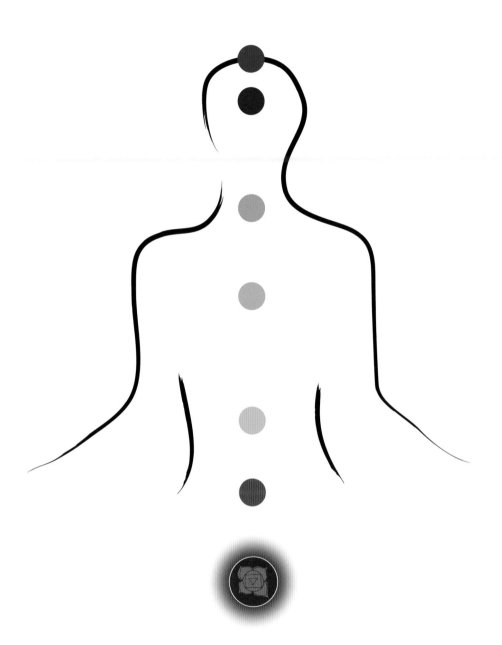

"I AM"

Day 1

THE ROOT CHAKRA

THE ROOT CHAKRA IS
YOUR ENERGETIC
FOUNDATION. IT IS
CONCERNED WITH ALL
MATTERS OF EARTHLY
EXISTENCE SUCH AS
FOOD, SHELTER, SAFETY,
PROSPERITY, TRUST,
AND FAMILY.

WELCOME TO THE FIRST DAY OF YOUR CLEANSE! This day of the Root is all about grounding, feeling safe and secure, and maintaining a sturdy base. Your innate knowledge, your bodily wisdom, this amazing vehicle serving as the magic carpet for riding through this life has all the answers you seek. Trust, respect, and listen to your organism.

We must root to rise. Everything has a foundation, from building a house to setting up a yoga posture. We must plug into the power source that is Earth in order to turn on and glow! Sit in a chair with your feet planted firmly on the ground, hands resting on your knees with palms facing up. Keep your spine straight for the spine is the line to the divine.

Take everything in, be an aware observer, learner, and lover of your process and life. You are on a curative pathway. First beautify your soul's home, then your block, community, city, country, world, and universe. One by one, tended soul gardens spread and inspire.

Visualize sending red taproots down into the earth, cracking through the floor, the carpet, rug, wood, cement, plumbing, Earth's crust, tectonic plates, and molten lava until your root tendrils wrap around the core of the planet. Be truly present in your body.

Now stand on your two feet. Stability and strength come natural to you. Find your center by pressing the soles of your feet into the earth as you press the palms of your hands together at your navel. Sway a little to experience being off center, and then find your way back home. Now bend and leap, run in place, feel your muscles and bones working together to move you as you draw sustenance from your deep roots.

BE BAREFOOT

Feel the earth beneath your feet, knowing you are connected to and supported by the planet in all areas of life. If it feels right for you, take this day to experience many different textures by walking on grass, sand, pebbles, and more.

Giant trees must have strong and secure root systems in order to grow tall, branch out, and flourish. The sturdy trunk structure provides the container for nutrients to flow from root to fruit and back. This is also true of our own bodies, skin and bones serving as the fleshly boundary so that the inner workings and energy within may be limitless.

Break out the potting soil and plant root vegetables, lettuces, herbs, flowers, or succulents. Take note there is a season for every plant, emotion, action, and reaction. Play in the dirt by making mud pies or go to the beach and build sand castles! Engage with nature by lying on a huge sun soaked boulder or the grass in a yard or park. Acknowledging the connectivity of humans and our Mother Earth is integral to our thriving. A healthy planet translates to happy people.

Bathe in nature! Combat confusion with countrysides, tackle tension with trees, and dump depression in the desert. Take a hike or walk and dedicate a portion of your journey to picking up any garbage that may be in your pathway. Not only will you be beautifying your neighborhood and honoring your home but probably saving a bird from having a belly full of styrofoam or plastic.

Experience this as a meditation of cleaning up your life which is exactly what you're doing by embarking upon this cleanse—taking care of your body and the planet. No more carbonated sugar water filled plastic bottles or empty calorie laden chip bag wrappers in your way. You are sweeping your side of the street and starting a ChakWave of good in the world!

THE CAVE YOU FEAR TO ENTER
HOLDS THE TREASURE YOU SEEK.

—Joseph Campbell

Once back home, clean and organize your physical desk or perhaps your computer desktop. Trash, recycle, and attend to tasks that have previously been pushed aside. As the Root Chakra deals with our earthly situations, take the time to tidy up your home. With every object you dust, remove, or repair, visualize yourself clearing a block within. A person's space can be a reflection of their life. Many times where there is cluttered chaos on the outside, this is the case inside as well.

Even if it's just one cupboard that is focused on today, take the time to scrub and scour and carefully place only items that are useful, beautiful, or sentimental in this newly grounded area. You may also want to rearrange your furniture or add artwork which truly expresses the real you. Move energy, shed the old, and reinvent yourself by setting aside possessions for a yard or online sale. Organize your home to organize your life, and Feng shui your future!

Balancing the root chakra asks you to face your fears in order to step into the life you are meant to live. If not residing in a place of happiness and truth, changing your circumstances, situation, and point of view is vital. Consider and recognize situations of physical, mental, verbal, or systemic violence or abuse present in your life, and take action in removing yourself from these unhealthy scenarios.

Allow yourself to be free. So many times we keep ourselves in bondage and burden ourselves and others with limiting beliefs. We can all live abundantly, but sometimes a false sense of limitation dulls our potential as individuals and humanity as a whole. Shed rigid dogmas that smother your soul, and go in the direction of your heart, passion, love, and bliss.

The evolution of your soul is occurring, like it or not. You're gathering information and experiences all the time, further molding who you are. This can be scary stuff if you don't invite change in a healthy manner. Take it step by step, and don't be afraid to ask for assistance. You are amazing and remind the rest of us we are as well.

WHY TRY TO EXPLAIN MIRACLES TO YOUR KIDS WHEN YOU CAN JUST HAVE THEM PLANT A GARDEN?

— *Robert Brault*

Release the rut. Yes, when in a rut, you know where you are going, but what if you peeked outside the trench and the view was glorious? What if you decided to climb out and choose your own pathway? Magic may ensue!

Some believe the higher chakras are somehow more important than the lower ones, that a job done with the mind is more worthy than one done with the physical body, or that the heavens are more pure than the earth. But the sacred IS present on earth, in nature, in YOU. When you till the soil you till your soul.

Check Out Marie Kondo's *The Life-Changing Magic of Tidying Up: The Japanese Art of Decluttering and Organizing* outlining a joyfully structured system for those desiring to go deeply into the realm of tidying. www.konmari.com

For those with small children, Creating Calm's Christine O'Brien helps families create harmony at home by strengthening relationships and clearing clutter. www.creatingcalmcoach.com

You are
brilliant, and
the earth is
hiring.

—Paul Hawken

Sanskrit name:
Muladhara

Means:
Root Support

Mantra:
I AM

Color:
red

Location:
base of spine, perineum

Element:
earth

Sense:
smell

Areas of Body Influenced:
adrenal gland, colon, legs, feet, coccyx, anus, large intestine, bones

Meditation:
My foundation is solid, and I am safe. Trusting my instincts, I welcome stability and abundance. Rooted and centered, I ground to grow.

Lessons for the Spirit:
security, stability, safety, success, instincts, abundance, wellness, finances, loyalty, grounding, trust

Unbalanced:
fear, materialistic, laziness, weight issues, unhealthy relationship with food, superstitions, violence, poverty, barely surviving, anxious, apathetic toward living, unwilling to change

Balancing Activities:
gardening, cleaning, cooking, drumming, playing in the dirt, petting animals, organizing your home, walking barefoot, giving or receiving a massage, surrounding yourself with the color RED

Vibrational Sound:
Oh (as in rope)

Seed Sound:
LAM

Tonal Key:
C

Gems, Crystals, and Minerals:
ruby, red garnet, bloodstone, red jasper, black tourmaline, obsidian, smoky quartz, red coral, fire opal, rhodonite, hematite

Essential Oils:
cedar, clove, patchouli, frankincense, angelica, spikenard, vetiver

ChakWave Herbal Blend:
dandelion root, elderberries, astragalus, goji berries

THE ROOT CHAKRA: YOGA POSTURES

Tadasana
(Mountain Pose)

Vriksasana
(Tree Pose)

Parsvakonasana
(Side Angle Pose)

Utkatasana
(Chair Pose)

Adho Mukha Svanasana
(Downward Dog)

THE ROOT CHAKRA: RECIPE

Ingredients

8 medium beets

3 cups strawberries

5 apples

½ cup ChakWave herbal tea (optional)

2 teaspoons chia seeds (optional)

Directions

Brew the herbal tea and allow to cool. Juice the beets, strawberries (trim the greens off), and apples. Mix together and whisk in chia seeds.

If you prefer less sweetness, you may choose to juice just the beets. Drinking only water and/or herbal tea today is also an option.

THE ROOT CHAKRA: NUTRITION

Iron rich **BEETS** are literally red roots from the nourishing soil. A blood tonic increasing immune system functioning, lowering blood pressure and increasing flow, they are the ultimate Root Chakra food. Beets are filled with folate and contain betalaines, which aid in detoxification, digestion, and are used to treat depression. Rumor has it Aphrodite consumed beets for beauty!

Plump **STRAWBERRIES** contain riboflavin, vitamin B6, copper, zinc, and help in lowering cholesterol. There are about 200 seeds in a single strawberry, and tens of thousands of strawberries are served with dollops of cream each year at Wimbledon. In medieval times they symbolized peace, prosperity, and perfection, and "Strawberry Fields Forever" by The Beatles was inspired by John Lennon's days of playing in the garden of a Salvation Army children's home named "Strawberry Field."

Norse mythology holds **APPLES** as a source of eternal youth, and in many cultures they are associated with love, pleasure, sensuality, virility, and fertility. In 1904, fruit specialist J.T. Stinson declared, "an apple a day keeps the doctor away" at the St. Louis Exposition. Not only rich in lore, they are rich in antioxidants and alkalinity keeping pH levels balanced. Apples are dipped in honey during Rosh Hashanah, the Jewish New Year, to symbolize the sweetness of life. Their round shape also serves as a reminder of seasonal and life cycles, of coming full circle.

Earthy and immune boosting **DANDELION ROOT** provides potassium and is a diuretic which rids the body of excess fluids. It was used by Native Americans to clear the skin and by the Chinese as a blood purifier. Dandelions are nicknamed "fairy clocks" as their flowers open in the morning and close at night in a timely manner.

A staple in Ayurvedic medicine, toxin-eliminating **ASTRAGALUS** is an adaptogen which helps the body resist stress and find balance. Used as a rejuvenating rasayana, a tonic for greater vitality and longevity, astragalus helps tissues stay healthy and may slow the aging process. Supportive of the adrenals and immune system, this powerhouse herb combats anemia, allergies, and cancer.

ELDERBERRY treats colds, flu and has anti-inflammatory, antiviral, and anticancer properties. Elderwood is used to make woodwind instruments and is said to create music the spirit world appreciates, connecting the physical to the spiritual.

GOJI BERRIES, also called wolfberries, have amino acids, potassium, and antioxidants galore. In China they are planted to help control erosion of the Earth, and in a sense they also help in preventing erosion of the body as they contain polysaccharides, which support the immune system.

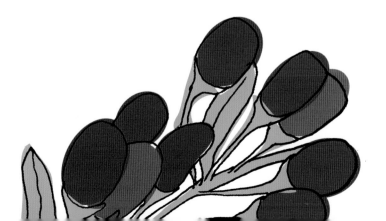

THE ROOT CHAKRA: JOURNAL PROMPT

I AM . . .

Scan your body. How do you feel right now? Where do these feelings reside? Acknowledge any pains or pleasures physically, mentally, emotionally, and spiritually.

_____

_____

_____

_____

_____

Write or draw a "body map" of your current state examining the structure of your self and life. Explore your consciousness and where you feel energy moving freely or where it is blocked.

_____

_____

_____

_____

_____

Contemplate how you handle change. Do you hoard, engage in workaholism, reside in fear? How grounded, healthy, and secure in your family and finances do you feel?

_____

_____

_____

_____

_____

What is your relationship to your fleshly form (i.e. gratitude, disgust, weight complaints, etc)? What are you noticing while drinking the juices you have prepared for today (i.e. elimination, constipation, hunger, lightness, etc.)? Take a moment to be amazed by the intricate workings of your body.

_____

_____

_____

_____

_____

Walk as if you are
kissing the Earth
with your feet.

—Thich Nhat Hanh

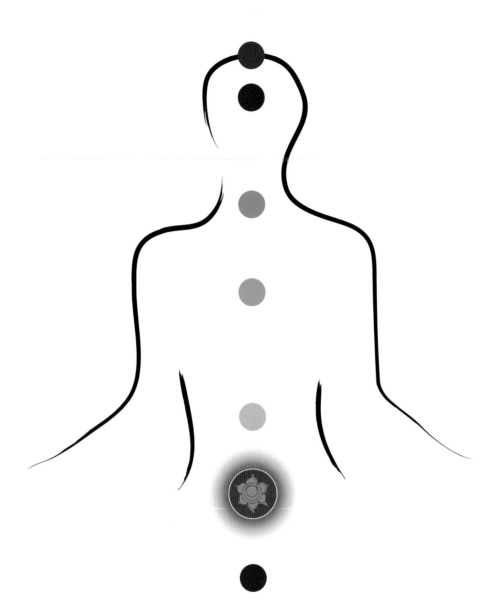

"I CREATE"

Day 2

THE SACRAL
CHAKRA

THE SACRAL CHAKRA IS YOUR SENSUAL CENTER. CREATIVITY, RELATIONSHIPS, DESIRE, PLEASURE, SEXUALITY, AND JOY ARE CONNECTED TO THIS CHAKRA.

IT'S SENSUAL SACRAL TIME! Once grounded in Root's earthiness, the Sacral Chakra's creative energy is invited to flow freely. This sexy, sacred center is our bed of creativity. It is the area of the body we materialized in and emerged from . . . and the same place where creative ideas, passionate emotions, and frolicking play are birthed!

Allow your feelings to flood your body and soul while sipping this spicy, creamy cocktail where the orange, cantaloupe, and carrot mingle as cinnamon, cayenne, and paprika tingle! We are water filled creatures. Liquids are the source of our vitality. Circulation, menstruation, ovulation, urination, semen, tears, breast milk, and mucus are the juices of life. Fluids follow the pathway of least resistance, rivers carving into land or tears streaming down a cheek.

Embrace your sea legs and sensuality. Shake off cobwebs by rolling your hips, summoning a belly dancer's sensuality. Turn on some sultry tunes, and dance a dance of desire as you weave and bob, dipping and diving throughout your home. Explore the feelings in your gyrating body of water. Allow yourself to let loose, get playful, and "swim" throughout the space.

MAN IS MOST NEARLY HIMSELF
WHEN HE ACHIEVES THE
SERIOUSNESS OF A CHILD AT PLAY.

— *Heraclitus*

Fold your body forward, releasing tension and emotions caught in your hips. Bend one knee and then the other letting go of stress, strain, and shame. Dangle your head down and shake out your locks. Consider taking the show on the road and going out into the world to dance . . . in a club, class, friend's home, park, or on a beach perhaps.

Solid relationships with yourself and others are key to a healthy Sacral chakra, and jealousy is often a demon that needs to be addressed. If people you perceive to have beauty, riches, success, love, and happiness bring up sadness or anger inside you, practice shifting your mindset into a place of "Wow, if s/he has that . . . so can I!"

This helps us to exist in a healthier, happier space. When able to genuinely admire, respect, and congratulate others we open up a free flowing exchange of energy and ideas. There is no point in keeping each other down because there is room for all of us to thrive. Access emotions, embrace vulnerability, and take risks!

EXPRESS YOURSELF,
DON'T REPRESS YOURSELF.

— *Madonna*

PERHAPS YOUR CHALLENGE ISN'T
FINDING A BETTER PROJECT OR A
BETTER BOSS. PERHAPS YOU NEED
TO GET IN TOUCH WITH WHAT
IT MEANS TO FEEL PASSIONATE.
PEOPLE WITH PASSION LOOK FOR
WAYS TO MAKE THINGS HAPPEN.

—*Seth Godin*

Invite a friend, lover, or even a stranger to play with you. Practice giving and living harmoniously by shadowing each other's movements. Take turns leading and following, offering and receiving. Interact and work together in creative movement making, listening and reacting.

Sex is one of life's amazing ways to express and connect. The reproductive area is sensitive . . . physically, emotionally, and culturally. This is where our flesh opens up to the outside world in order to receive and give understanding and pleasure.

An incredibly powerful force, our sexual nature brings people together. It is also a sensitive area for we have created stories around sexuality, genders, orientations, and persuasions. Sexism, ignorance, violence, oppression, and stigmas are rampant in the world. Every word and action counts. Instead of calling names or placing blames, let's celebrate, uplift, and encourage safe, healthy sexuality for all.

Set aside time at home to soak in a sensual bath. Break out the bubbles, detoxifying salts, healing herbs, orange colored bath powder, aromatic oils, and buttery body washes. Luxuriously bathe yourself and take pleasure in the pampering. Care for yourself so you may care for others. By filling your proverbial cup, you have the ability to "runneth over" nourishing and helping others rather than dipping down into your energetic well. If you run yourself ragged for an extended time, the well dries up and you are unable to enjoy the juiciness of life.

Water can be still, calm, bubbling, flowing, rushing, pulsating, or crushing just like energy and emotions. As water cleanses the body, allow it to also cleanse your mind and soul. Remove the dirt of selfishness, shame, pain, envy, and ill will so your pure self may emerge making the navigation of life's winding waterways more effortless.

STAND LIKE MOUNTAIN,
MOVE LIKE WATER.

—*Ancient Chinese Proverb*

H2 . . . OH HOW WE LOVE WATER! Cool, clear, clean water is vital for life. Three quarters of the planet is covered with it, and our bodies are comprised of essentially the same ratio. We can surf on it, dive into it, and drink it down. This indispensable element bathes us inside and out.

Find a water source today. An ocean, sea, lake, pond, river, brook, creek, waterfall, water park, swimming pool, or bathtub will do the trick. Being beside water or, even better, IN water welcomes you into the womb of the earth; here you are in touch with the natural and elegant fluid part of you which connects to all beings.

Submerge yourself in the life sustaining liquid and listen for the gurgles within your own watery body. Float and splash in the same water your ancestors swam in and drank from, the same waters where fish make their home and animals gather.

Relationships are assignments for optimal growth and healing.

—*Gabrielle Bernstein*

Sanskrit name:
Svadhisthana

Meaning:
Sweetness

Mantra:
I CREATE

Color:
orange

Location:
lower abdomen

Element:
water

Sense:
taste

Areas of Body Influenced:
reproductive organs, ovaries and testis, womb, prostate, hips, sacrum, bladder, lower back, kidneys

Meditation:
I am creative and passionate, flowing fluidly through life. Welcoming pleasure and sensuality, I play and experience joy. I am an emotional being, present and aware of my feelings.

Lessons for the Spirit:
creation, transformation, intimacy, vitality, flow, forgiveness, sexuality, connectivity, enthusiasm, passion, enjoyment, surrender

Unbalanced:
guilt, shame, jealousy, moodiness, sexual abuse, violence, addictions, over-indulgence in or lack of desire for sex, repression, oppression, purposelessness, unquenchable desires, lack of trust

Balancing Activities:
dancing, swimming, making love, self-pleasuring, hula-hooping, yogic hip openers, expressing creativity, having fun, caressing, tickling, taking a bath, surrounding yourself with the color ORANGE

Vibrational Sound:
OO (as in rule)

Seed Sound:
VAM

Tonal Key:
D

Gems, Crystals, and Minerals:
moonstone, carnelian, topaz, orange calcite, tiger's eye, amber, coral, peach aventurine, orange jasper, selenite

Essential Oils:
ylang ylang, bergamot, cardamom, clary sage, neroli, orange, cinnamon

ChakWave Herbal Blend:
calendula flower, passion flower, cinnamon bark

THE SACRAL CHAKRA: YOGA POSTURES

Eka Pada Rajakapotasana
(Pigeon Pose)

Baddha Konasana
(Bound Angle Pose)

Utkata Konasana
(Goddess Pose)

Uttanasana
(Standing Forward Bend)

Virabhadrasana II
(Warrior II)

THE SACRAL CHAKRA: RECIPE

Ingredients

1 cantaloupe

3 oranges

12 carrots

1 teaspoon paprika powder

1 teaspoon cayenne pepper powder

½ cup ChakWave herbal tea (optional)

2 teaspoons chia seeds (optional)

Directions

Brew the herbal tea and allow to cool while juicing the cantaloupe (remove the rind), oranges (remove most of the peel or use a citrus juicer), and carrots (remove the greens). Mix all liquids together, and whisk in paprika, cayenne, and chia seeds.

If you prefer less sweetness, you may choose to juice just the carrots. Drinking only water and/or herbal tea today is also an option.

THE SACRAL CHAKRA: NUTRITION

These awesome orbs increase the metabolic rate, help build and repair cells, and have anti-inflammatory properties which can reduce arthritis. Containing vitamin C (which aids in the production of anti-aging collagen) galore, **ORANGES** rock potassium, magnesium, thiamin, and folate too. During Chinese New Year it is tradition to set out oranges for good health, wealth, and a long life.

Carotenoids in **CARROTS** such as beta-carotene support the kidneys, skin, and mucous membranes. They promote healthy cell growth and protect from uterine, prostate, and bladder cancers. Vitamin A is a hormone helper, and women's sexual responsiveness receives a boost as does the health of the womb. These phallic shaped vegetables assist in the production and motility of a man's sperm, and speaking of sexy, ladies of the English court wore lacy carrot top foliage as hair and hat ornamentation.

This marvelous melon embodies all things Sacral by being fabulously fleshy and wonderfully watery. **CANTALOUPE** has vitamins C and A, and they provide antioxidants, anticoagulants, and are anticarcinogenic. These potassium rich melons picked up their name from the Italian town of Cantalupo in Sabina which literally means "singing wolves" while in Australia and New Zealand they are usually called rockmelons due to their exterior similar to that of a rock.

Chinese medical philosophy credits **CINNAMON** with removing blocks causing pain and cramps by moving vital chi energy. Its warming affect heats up cold extremities for finger and toe titillating pleasure all the while reducing blood sugar, blood pressure, and LDL cholesterol. Cinnamon improves circulation to the abdomen relieving discomfort, supports the uterus, and combats bladder and yeast infections. Its aroma boosts memory and cognitive function, and in the Middle Ages as a symbol of wealth, cinnamon was served to impress guests.

Stunning **PASSION FLOWER** has been used as an aphrodisiac by the Aztecs, Mayans, and Native Americans. When this tenacious vine is not weaving its way to the top of rainforest canopies and enhancing sexual desire, it calms nervous energy, lowers blood pressure, eases menstrual cramps, and promotes relaxation with its natural serotonin.

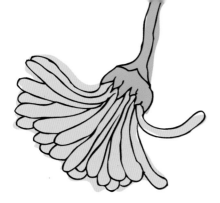

As an anti-inflammatory, **CALENDULA FLOWER** boosts the libido and helps in balancing reproductive hormones. It supports uterine and abdominal health, helps repair tissue, and aides in digestion. Used topically, this beautifully bright bloom helps heal skin of everything from eczema to burns, varicose veins to diaper rash. A bath of calendula tea soothes postpartum inflammation and reduces hemorrhoids.

Pungent **PAPRIKA** made of powdered peppers provides vitamin A for happy cells, veins, capillaries, and bright, glowing skin. An anti-inflammatory, it helps relieve swelling. It also pumps up production of saliva and stomach acids for smooth digestion. In the cosmetic realm, paprika is sometimes mixed with henna to color hair.

Hot and spicy **CAYENNE** is a popular weight loss tool because it contains capcaicin which speeds up the metabolism. Making mucous membranes catch fire is a specialty of this chili pepper, and those whom find pleasure in the fiery pain experience euphoric endorphin rushes. Increased body heat and blood flow gives energy levels a boost so dash a double dose!

THE SACRAL CHAKRA:
JOURNAL PROMPT

I CREATE . . .

Creative Kundalini energy is often represented by a coiled serpent awaiting activation. Visualize a snake trapped in a lidded aquarium filled with water. The snake is trying to find an escape by poking her head out of corners. Determined, she knows she must find freedom to survive. What ways in your life are you and your creative powers like this boxed snake?

_____

_____

_____

_____

_____

How can you facilitate the rising of your Kundalini energy? What are your passions? What is it you need to heal and want to create here in this world? What old skin or habits do you need to shed in order to move forward?

_____

_____

_____

_____

_____

Like that boxed up Kundalini snake, your time in the box is limited. How will you say YES to the adventure into your destiny? Allow your creativity to flow, flourish, and break free.

_____

_____

_____

_____

_____

SACRED ORGASMIC DANCE

A combination of ceremonial and 5 elements
dance, shamanic healing, tantra, yoga, tribal, Indian,
African, breath work, voice releasing and chakra shaking,
Acqua Xena Heart helps participants to release trauma,
fear, shame, guilt, and pain and to tap into their leadership,
ecstasy, power and freedom.
www.sacredorgasmicdance.com

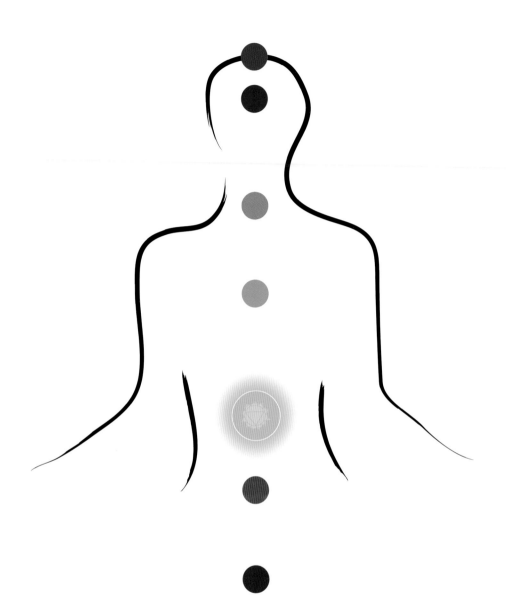

"I CAN"

Day 3

THE SOLAR PLEXUS CHAKRA

THE SOLAR PLEXUS CHAKRA IS OUR POWER CENTER. IT IS THE ENGINE THAT PROPELS YOU FORWARD WITH STRENGTH, COURAGE, SELF-ESTEEM, SELF-RESPECT, AND SELF-DISCIPLINE.

HERE COMES THE SOLAR PLEXUS SuN LiTTLE DAHHHLiNG!

This is the jeweled city where fiery golden light fills the soul with discipline, order, and virtue. Just above the navel, the Manipura power center is the digestive control room. This is where you literally digest food as well as assimilate necessary emotional nutrients for life, energy, form, and focus.

Plants are sun powered. The sun shines, plants grow, and we gratefully ingest vital solar energy. Summon the sun. Visualize the burning orb in your belly, emanating pure energy from your life force furnace. Allow the blazing flames to ignite you, motivate you to take action, and resist resistance. The Solar Plexus element is fire, and humans are the only animals with fire. Stoke it!

This "fire in the belly" courageous core is where intention meets energy to propel the life engine forward. You may intend to find that perfect career or partner, but if you're not engaging with the world and taking action, it's unlikely these desires will come into fruition. The same goes for energy without intention. If you have energy coursing through the veins but structure and focus have not been developed, goals will rarely be met. Your true power is experienced when you are able to do difficult things with graceful strength.

A GOAL IS A DREAM WITH A DEADLINE.

—Napoleon Hill

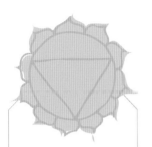

WRING OUT your abdominal organs by twisting round your middle. Like a wet rag, this core work compresses the organs. When released, they are flooded with freshly oxygenated blood. Lymphatic fluid is flushed, and digestion is stimulated with this toxin twist.

Play with fire. Light a candle, fireplace, or bonfire! Gaze at the flames, and feel the heat. Be a warrior burning through obstacles and frustrations. Take a "Breath of Fire Break" keeping the tummy taut and pumping rapid breaths out of your nose. Will yourself through fatigue. Make tight fists and a cheerleader's "V" of outstretched arms on the exhale. Bend your elbows and bring them into your core on the inhale. Challenge yourself to follow through for five minutes. Keep on keeping on just like the sun.

When the primal pit of your stomach gives you a heads up, that's your instinctive "gut feeling." This is your body's brain, and the body doesn't lie. These spontaneous feelings hold deep, visceral, first response wisdom. Listening and responding is a skill that takes time to hone and honor. Immediate responses are where primal, personal truth resides. Heed the messages, go with your gut, and use your power for good.

PLAYING IT SAFE IS THE RISKIEST CHOICE WE CAN EVER MAKE.

—Sarah Ban Breathnach

When the Solar Plexus is unbalanced, feelings are brushed aside or completely ignored out of intended politeness, an inability to interpret signals, or not wanting to rock the proverbial boat. Doubt, anxiety, lethargy, fear of criticism, and the inability to make decisions takes hold. Own your power and potential.

On the other side of the pendulum, an out-of-control Solar Plexus leads to an inflated ego, ruthlessness, greed, fanaticism, and violence. Finding the balance in valuing ourselves while serving others with integrity and respect is the sweet spot. By doing the personal work to become the most honest version of [insert your name here], YOU are able to lead without employing force or coercion.

Embody assertiveness and self-esteem so you may act on intuition, and practice making steadfast decisions. They don't have to be huge. As with working out, these are muscles to be built, and the results do not happen overnight. But progress and success are readily available to you if you stick to your personal plan.

Respect healthy boundaries. Push other boundaries. Break through your boundaries. Claim your right to exist, release being meek, and confront challenges. You are not a doormat. Practice saying "No" to things that seep and scatter energy and time from your days or hinder you from discovering and acting upon your truest callings. On the flip side, steer clear of being a bully. Aggressive threats and intimidating tactics are harmful and help no one. Find the assertive center ground to stand in your power.

What frightens you? Consider doing it. Throw attachment and aversion into the metaphorical flames, using them to fuel your internal fires. Take a risk, and decide to decide. Confidence, concentration, and control lead to transformation. The universe needs you to take control, rise to your full potential, and freely give your gifts.

EVERYTHING YOU WANT IS OUT THERE WAITING FOR YOU TO ASK. EVERYTHING YOU WANT ALSO WANTS YOU. BUT YOU HAVE TO TAKE ACTION TO GET IT.

—Jack Canfield

Think of this entire cleanse as a willpower bootcamp for you as you stay consciously present and committed to your growth and health, while not dipping into the chocolate stash. Try controlling the remote control in your household. What is it YOU would like to watch? Or post an article you resonate with but fear may offend others on the social media platform of your choice. Sometimes it takes great courage to click "share."

After your cleanse, build this muscle of independence by making definite decisions when ordering from a menu. Don't hem and haw and ponder if it's soup or salad you would like. Experience the feeling of making a choice and sticking to it. Practice makes powerful. Making "small" decisions confidently builds up toward the "big" ones such as choosing romantic or business partners that may affect your long term well-being.

Keep your face always toward the sunshine— and shadows will fall behind you.

—Walt Whitman

Greatness is the
courage to overcome
obstacles.

— David R. Hawkins

Sanskrit name
Manipura

Meaning
Lustrous Gem

Mantra
I CAN

Color
yellow

Location
abdomen, navel

Element
fire

Sense
sight

Areas of Body Influenced
liver, stomach, pancreas, diaphragm, gallbladder, adrenal glands, spleen, small intestine, digestive tract

Meditation
I am courageous and powerful, burning through obstacles. I radiate confidence as my commitment and willpower help me to achieve my goals. I am strong, worthy, and whole.

Lessons for the Spirit
personal power, willpower, vitality, self-esteem, self-image, responsibility, purpose, strength, effectiveness, dedication, independence, leadership

Unbalanced
low self-esteem, weak will, critical thoughts, anxiety, perfectionism, anger, frustration, blaming, sluggishness, passivity, overbearing, lack of self-discipline, authoritarian, status obsessed, power hungry, unhealthy need for recognition, victim mentality, destructive desire for material possessions

Balancing Activities
taking action, soaking up the sun, belly laughing, gazing at a flame or fire, sit ups, core strengthening exercises, Pranayama breath work, playing a competitive sport, surrounding yourself with the color YELLOW

Vibrational Sound
Ah (as in God)

Seed Sound
RAM

Tonal Key
E

Gems, Crystals, and Minerals
citrine, sunstone, gold citrine, gold topaz, amber, tiger's eye, peridot, yellow tourmaline, yellow jasper, iron pyrite

Essential Oils
peppermint, lemon, lemon balm, juniper berry, basil, geranium, jasmine

ChakWave Herbal Blend
marshmallow root, chamomile flower, tulsi leaf

THE SOLAR PLEXUS CHAKRA: YOGA POSTURES

Navasana
(Boat Pose)

Kumbhakasana
(Plank Pose)

Vasisthasana
(Side Plank Pose)

Virabhadrasana I
(Warrior I Pose)

Parivrtta Trikonasana
(Revolved Triangle Pose)

THE SOLAR PLEXUS CHAKRA: RECIPE

Ingredients

3 pineapples (about 9 cups chopped pineapple)

6 inches ginger (about 6 tablespoons . . . or be generous
   and add more to your spicy liking!)

3 inches turmeric root (or 3 teaspoons turmeric powder)

½ cup ChakWave herbal tea (optional)

2 teaspoons chia seeds (optional)

Directions

Brew the herbal tea and allow to cool. Juice the ginger, turmeric, and pineapples. Mix liquids and whisk in chia seeds.

If you prefer less sweetness, you may choose to juice just ginger and/or turmeric. Enjoy as a powerful shot or add water. Drinking only water and/or herbal tea today is also an option.

THE MOST EFFECTIVE WAY I have found to cut pineapples for juicing is to lay the fruit on its side and chop off the spiky crown and base, then turn upright like a column, rotating and slicing the spiny skin off from top to bottom. Don't worry if there is some skin or spots left on the sides as your juicer will separate the solids from liquids. Still standing up, cut down the center of the pineapple creating two halves. Cut each half in half lengthwise as well, and then slice horizontally three times so that you create long pineapple pieces.

As juicer openings vary, these may fit perfectly or you may need to cut them down to a thinner width. Go ahead and use the hard core portion as your juicer will extract the juicy goodness from even the densest areas.

THE SOLAR PLEXUS CHAKRA: NUTRITION

High levels of manganese in **PINEAPPLES** gives a potent energy boost while the enzyme bromelain breaks down proteins and serves as an anti-inflammatory, collagen builder, and weight loss aide. Regarded as exotic and luxurious, pineapples have been used as symbols of hospitality and homecoming for centuries.

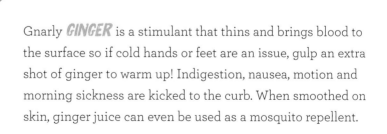

Gnarly **GINGER** is a stimulant that thins and brings blood to the surface so if cold hands or feet are an issue, gulp an extra shot of ginger to warm up! Indigestion, nausea, motion and morning sickness are kicked to the curb. When smoothed on skin, ginger juice can even be used as a mosquito repellent.

An antispasmodic which helps reduce plaque buildup in arteries, *TURMERIC* strengthens the digestive system, liver, and pancreas. Always interestingly shaped, turmeric (along with ginger) is a rhizome, which is Greek for "mass of roots." In India where turmeric is widely cultivated and used for everything from relieving gas to dying fabrics, there are over fifty Sanskrit words describing this revered root.

The sugary s'mores type of marshmallows found in the supermarket today were once made using actual mucilaginous *MARSHMALLOW ROOT,* which is a stomach pleaser and protector. By coating and moistening mucous membranes, ulcers and indigestion head for the hills. Marshmallow got a shout out in Homer's Iliad as a prized healing herb, and the raw roots can even be used as a soothing teething ring for babies.

CHAMOMILE FLOWER is a classic comforting carminative that calms all things gastrointestinal and troublesome to the tummy. It promotes relaxation and restfulness and assuages menstrual cramps and pain associated with childbirth. Ancient Egyptians associated the yellow flower with the power of the sun.

Known as the "Queen of Herbs" in India, **TULSI** calms energy, combats sugar cravings, and levels blood sugar. An adaptagen, tulsi supports the body in maintaining wellness and keeping stress at bay. The leaves relieve constipation, gas, bloating, acidity, and ulcers. Revered by many Hindus as a healing goddess in plant form, when tulsi migrated from East to West it picked up the name "Holy Basil."

THE SOLAR PLEXUS CHAKRA:
JOURNAL PROMPT

I CAN . . .

What's something that's been lingering on your "to do" list for ages? How about something you would like to achieve or complete in life? Why are you putting it off?

_____

_____

_____

_____

_____

Fear of rejection or humiliation, or doubting whether we are worthy or good enough are often the culprits. Give names to the obstacles you face and determine how you will overcome them. Chances are you are expending more energy fretting about not doing the big IT than you would if you just finished it already!

_____

_____

_____

_____

_____

Remember the maxim of "one foot in front of the other" and break down the big picture goal into attainable action steps for today, tomorrow, and the next day.

_____

_____

_____

_____

_____

There is no superior telling you to get back to work on your life's mission so take care to make detailed plans in order to avoid laziness or procrastination.

Completing commitments strengthens resolution. Claim your right to be the leader of your life, knowing you are capable of truly manifesting destiny. P.S. You are awesome.

_____

_____

_____

_____

_____

INTENTIONAL GOAL SETTING

Have an allergy to To-Do lists? Perhaps you already do way too much. Try clearing out the old do-do-do strategies so you may make way for feeling powerful, ambitious, and relaxed at the same time.

The process of Intentional Goal Setting is all about being "better than done" by focusing on who you want TO BE and then tracking evidence as your intentions become real. Less doing, more BEING, and lots of deep satisfaction to celebrate along the way. Check out Geffen Rothe's book at BetterThanDone.com and more power to you!

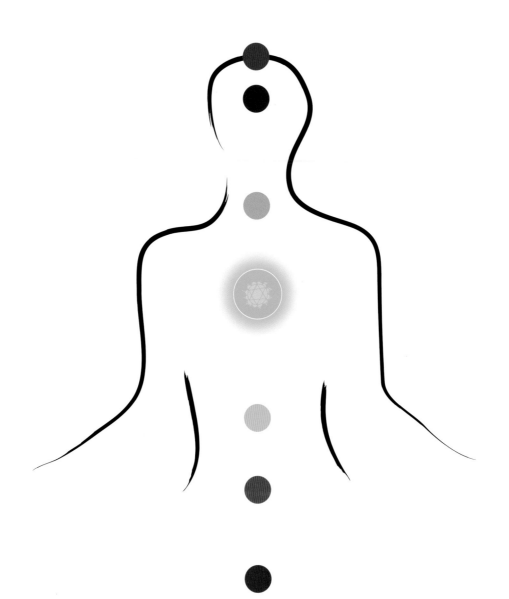

"I LOVE"

Day 4

THE HEART CHAKRA

THE HEART CHAKRA IS
YOUR CENTER OF LOVE
AND COMPASSION. IT
CONNECTS THE LOWER
CHAKRAS TO THE HIGHER
CHAKRAS CREATING
A UNION RADIATING
UNCONDITIONAL LOVE.

LOVE HEALS THE HEART. Connecting and balancing, the Heart Chakra is located in the center of the chest and symbolized by two intersecting triangles. This is the center chakra where matter marries spirit. It is the integration of emotions and intellect, feminine and masculine, earth and heaven.

The Heart Chakra governs marriage, partnership, and commitment of all types. Being in relationship, we are asked to be completely honest, no hiding or holding back. The cobwebbed corners of half-truths or denials must be swept out and illuminated. Loving a parent, spouse, child, friend, pet, or other is a way of extending and expanding the heart outside our own selves. This reminds us that we are a web of interconnected organisms.

When opening the heart to true, universal love of your self, others, your mission, and life . . . forgiveness, compassion, and harmony are not only possible but inevitable. It is profound and beautiful to allow yourself to be truly open.

Vulnerability is courageous. And yes, being vulnerable has its risks and requires strength and stamina, but a life without connection to others is not a healthy or natural way to spend our time on earth.

Take the time to ask how someone is doing. This may be a loved one or a person on a park bench. Really listen to their story. Implement empathy and compassion without judgment or pity, and allow your heart to melt for humanity.

THE MINUTE A PERSON WHOSE WORD MEANS A GREAT DEAL TO OTHERS DARES TO TAKE THE OPEN-HEARTED AND COURAGEOUS WAY, MANY OTHERS FOLLOW.

—*Marian Anderson*

Luxuriate in another's presence, and allow yourself to be in awe of love. When down in the dumps, this is an especially nice practice to remind us everyone isn't "out to get us."

Sadness happens; it's a part of life's journey and a great teacher if we allow it to move through us. Heartache and grief are arguably the most intense feelings a person may bear. When we experience an intense trauma, the loss of a loved one, a break up, major letdown, or humiliation, retreat is a natural response. Broken trust can send us into self-preservation mode.

Energetic daggers in the heart are incredibly painful emotionally as well as physically. Stress creates cortisol, which hurts the heart muscle . . . so one can actually die of a broken heart. Release turmoil with crying, screaming, exercising, laughing, time in nature and with friends, extinguishing the "heart attack" and allowing love to permeate the protective armor.

If one is attracted to unhealthy relationships while pushing away potentially good ones, do the personal work in order to acknowledge and release old hurts, pains, fears, and biases you may be bringing to the table. To the best of your ability, get right with your own heart before embarking upon another relationship.

HEART ON YOUR SLEEVE HAND AND ARM SCRUB:

Be extra kind to your hands and arms today by treating yourself to a manicure or mixing up this simple scrub to slough off the old and soften up. Massage into skin, rinse, and reach out and touch someone.

- 2 parts coconut oil to 1 part sugar
- a few drops of the essential oil of your choice

We all have wounds to address and heal in this life, and when we heal ourselves we become a healing presence to others. When in doubt, forgive . . . yourself, your parents, your friends, your enemies, people you have never met. Reach out, apologize, send out tendrils of love, go all in because there's really no time for anything else. When cleared from the inside out we give the Universe room to work magic and present us with amazing opportunities.

Your breath is an incredibly powerful energy, and the element associated with the Heart Chakra is air so it's no wonder when our hearts are full of love we feel like we are "walking on air!" Hunch your shoulders inward and try finding your breath. In this constricted posture, it doesn't work too well. Shallow breathing and asthma are symptoms of underdeveloped heart health. Now roll your shoulders back, sitting straight and feeling the space created. You may feel instantly more open to giving and receiving. Slow, deep, long breaths are the key to balancing and attracting love.

Now for some energetic open heart surgery on yourself. Think of a limiting belief you have, a pattern that doesn't serve you anymore, or an action you perpetuate that is downright annoying. Breathe it in, and let it permeate your body. Feel the sensations, however uncomfortable, and hold it in until you are about to burst. Now spew it out, emptying your lungs and breathing in the fresh new expansiveness. This is a form of Tonglen, the Tibetan practice of breathing in pain, your pain and the pain of others. We must go to the places within where we are harboring grief, shame, loneliness, resentment, anger and all the "ugly" stuff in order to be able to let it go.

Now reverse the process. Breathe in the positive, the beautiful, the compassionate. Exhale the hurt, the outdated, the story you may be living that no longer serves you. This steady flow of breath in and out helps to purify the body. Beyond our personal stories of

TO LOVE ONESELF IS THE BEGINNING OF A LIFELONG ROMANCE.

—Oscar Wilde

METTA MEDITATION

Sit comfortably and relax into a Metta meditation of living loving-kindness. Bring your hands to your chest and feel the rise and fall of your breath. Bend your fingers inward so that the pads touch your chest. Begin gently "raking" outward from your heart center as you visualize your heart expanding. If in a negative mindset, make a conscious decision to shift into the gear of happiness and unconditional love.

Send well wishes and love to your partner, parents, siblings, children, cousins, aunts and uncles, friends, the closest people to you. When you are ready, grow the circle of love to include co-workers and everyone you know. Once you feel complete in that, widen the meditation to those you do not know, those you have tension with, your community, town, state, country, continent, hemisphere, world, universe and beyond.

heartbreak and sadness there is a knowing that we are infinite and whole. When we have cleared the hurts and griefs from the past, this is where the unstruck, unstuck, unhurt, unharmed and freeing air element of the Anahata Chakra comes into play.

A stick of incense burns in one place, but we smell it all around because air seeks balance. When we light the Solar Plexus fire, airy Heart provides the fuel. Put a match or candle flame to a bundle of smudging sage, sweetgrass, lavender, palo santo, and/or cedar, and watch the smoke waft. Reverently focus your intention on clearing blocked energy and releasing your love into the world. When outside, enjoy wind chimes and breezes in the open air. Like love, air wants to expand and find its way into every nook and cranny.

The thymus, derived from the Greek word "thymos" meaning "life energy," is a gland in the chest which helps create equilibrium in the body. It does this by controlling the creation of white blood cells, which assist the body in fighting infection. It is also called the "happiness point" for when activated, the thymus can dissipate anxious energy, replacing it with calm vitality. While breathing deeply, try the "thymus thump" technique by using the index and middle finger knuckles to gently thump the center of your breastbone for about thirty seconds. Feel those endorphins spread throughout your body!

Your chest, arms, hands, and fingers are extensions of your heart. Let everything and everyone you touch be an act of love. Wear a green shirt or paint your nails green to remind yourself of this as you hold, touch, caress, exalt, honor, and hug it out! Open arms welcome open feelings of love and compassion, sharing and caring. In a hug from the heart, bodies intertwine and energies are melded. Turn "ughs" into "hugs" as you vibrate green love vibes.

DO WHAT YOU FEEL IN YOUR HEART TO BE RIGHT—FOR YOU'LL BE CRITICIZED ANYWAY.

—*Eleanor Roosevelt*

I am sorry
Please forgive me
Thank you
I love you

—Ho'o pono pono prayer

Sanskrit name
Anahata

Meaning
Unstruck or Unhurt

Mantra
I LOVE

Color
green (pink is also associated)

Location
chest

Element
air

Sense
touch

Areas of Body Influenced
heart, thymus, ribs, lungs, arms, hands, respiratory system, diaphragm, blood, circulatory system, cells, involuntary muscles

Meditation
I am kind to myself and others. Balanced and accepting, compassion is my first response. Filled with gratitude, I am love.

Lessons for the Spirit
divine love, peace, forgiveness, balance, empathy, acceptance, healing, harmony, surrender, compassion, hope, devotion, relationships

Unbalanced
prolonged grief, chronic sadness, loneliness, abandonment, resentment, hostility, co-dependency, demanding, possessiveness, martyrdom

Balancing Activities
helping, hugging, breathing exercises, flying a kite, shoulder rolls, arm extensions, backbends, writing a love letter, volunteering, breastfeeding, surrounding yourself with the colors GREEN and PINK

Vibrational Sound
Aye (long A)

Seed Sound
YAM

Tonal Key
F

Gems, Crystals, and Minerals
rose quartz, moss agate, jade, emerald, green aventurine, peridot, malachite, pink tourmaline, verdelite

Essential Oils
rose, rosemary, eucalyptus, bergamot, basil, thyme, yerba santa, elecampagne, oregano

ChakWave Herbal Blend
hawthorne berries, rose hips, rosemary

THE HEART CHAKRA: YOGA POSTURES

Urdhva Dhanurasana
(Wheel Pose)

Natarajasana
(King Dancer Pose)

Dhanurasana
(Bow Pose)

Setu Bandha Sarvangasana
(Bridge Pose)

Bhujangasana
(Cobra Pose)

THE HEART CHAKRA: RECIPE

10 cucumbers

15 leaves kale (about 2 bundles)

1 bundle peppermint

½ cup ChakWave herbal tea (optional)

2 teaspoons chia seeds (optional)

Directions

Brew herbal tea and allow to cool while juicing cucumbers (skins too!), kale, and peppermint.

Alternate placing the ingredients through the juicer as the watery cucumbers help in pushing the kale and peppermint through. Mix liquids and whisk in chia seeds.

Drinking only water and/or herbal tea today is also an option.

THE HEART CHAKRA: NUTRITION

Crunchy *CUCUMBERS* are ideal for juicing (or making dainty, cooling cucumber sandwiches) as these heartburn-relieving gourds are 90% water. Beneficial in healing lung and chest issues, cukes boast vitamin A, C, potassium, magnesium, and sterols, which lower cholesterol. Raw slices applied to skin reduce inflammation, swelling, and wrinkles with collagen firming phytochemicals. It is said Roman women desiring to become pregnant wore cucumbers around their waists in addition to using them in treating scorpion bites and bad eyesight.

The gorgeous green color of nutritionally dense and "heart-y" *KALE* is visually healing and harmonious. In the Celtic days of yore, the digging up of kale stalks was used to divine whom one would marry: the amount of dirt equaled dowry and the taste foretold traits of a future mate. Kale's calcium, folate, and iron work to reduce arterial plaque warding off heart disease. Indeed, green is good.

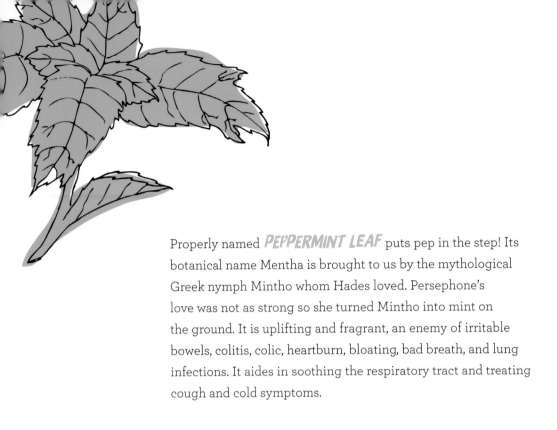

Properly named *PEPPERMINT LEAF* puts pep in the step! Its botanical name Mentha is brought to us by the mythological Greek nymph Mintho whom Hades loved. Persephone's love was not as strong so she turned Mintho into mint on the ground. It is uplifting and fragrant, an enemy of irritable bowels, colitis, colic, heartburn, bloating, bad breath, and lung infections. It aides in soothing the respiratory tract and treating cough and cold symptoms.

HAWTHORNE BERRIES are known as "tea for the heart" as they promote heart health and the circulation of blood throughout the body. The bioflavenoids help in relaxing and dilating arteries, which lowers blood pressure and helps reduce blood vessel degeneration. Bushes can grow up to 25 feet tall and live for hundreds of years. Some Christians believe the crown of thorns Jesus wore was made of hawthorne, and the Greeks associated the berries with fertility and marriage.

Get hip to the fruit of roses ... *ROSE HiPS!*
These seed filled pods are found beneath the
petals of the flower famously associated with romantic love.
During WWII shipments of citrus fruits were limited so Great
Britain's Ministry of Health distributed rose hip syrup as the
buds contain concentrated Vitamin C to fight colds and flus.
Rich in skin rejuvenating Vitamin A, rose hips heal wounds
and infections while reducing scar tissue, stretch marks, and
wrinkles.

"There's *ROSEMARY,* that's for remembrance; pray, love,
remember." Shakespeare's Ophelia in "Hamlet" knew what was
up as this aromatic herb strengthens the heart and increases
blood circulation, which leads to enhanced concentration and
memory. Symbolizing love and loyalty, rosemary is used at both
weddings and funerals. Antioxidants present in this evergreen
shrub protect one from cardiovascular disease and lessen
the effects of asthma. Traditional Chinese Medicine believes
rosemary fights fatigue by invigorating the flow of Qi energy.

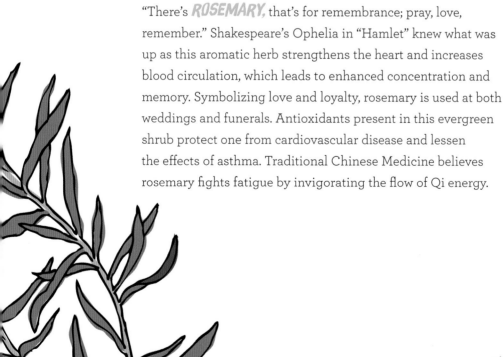

THE HEART CHAKRA: JOURNAL PROMPT

Write a love letter (or many!) to somebody or to yourself. Romantic
or not, allow your heart to speak making it 100% honest. Reveal your
feelings and express your gratitude. Gush in acknowledgement of
their gifts. Lie down with your shoulder blades flush against the earth
cradling your heart as you read your letter out loud.

_____

_____

_____

_____

_____

_____

_____

_____

_____

_____

_____

_____

_____

_____

_____

_____

_____

_____

_____

Have you played a part in causing pain in the life of another, or has someone hurt you deeply? Perhaps it is time to finally forgive yourself or another. Recognize this as a strong, bold choice. Take time to see seemingly unfortunate situations as opportunities for growth. This may help close a chapter and/or make room for a new beginning.

_____

_____

_____

_____

_____

_____

_____

_____

_____

_____

_____

_____

_____

_____

_____

_____

_____

_____

_____

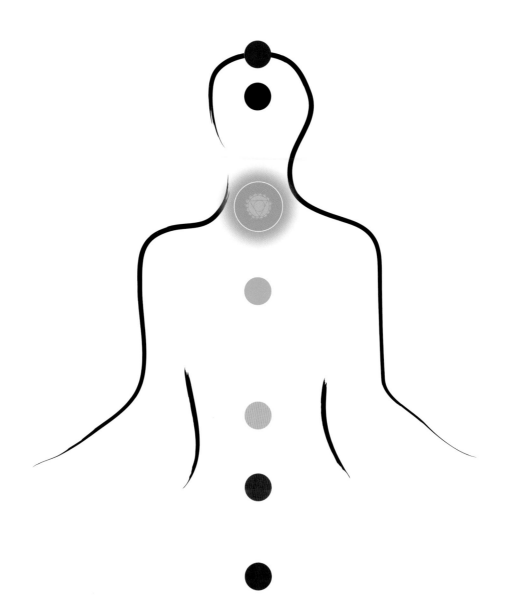

"I SPEAK"

Day 5

THE THROAT
CHAKRA

THE THROAT CHAKRA
IS YOUR CENTER
OF LISTENING
AND EXPRESSING.
INDIVIDUALITY,
COMMUNICATION,
PURIFICATION,
AND HONESTY
DWELL HERE.

LOCATED IN THE NARROWEST PASSAGEWAY OF THE CORE BODY, the Throat Chakra is the gateway for connection with others. This communication center is from where you speak, express, and listen. On this truthful day of the Throat, take a moment to sing a song (or yell or roar!) on your way to work, in the shower, or wherever you feel comfortable belting it out.

Check in with your Truth-o-meter. Are you fulfilled and living truthfully on a daily basis? Does your community nurture, excite, and thrill you? Are there areas of your life you can be more honest with yourself and others? Every day we head to work or hang out with friends or family, we trade "life time" for those experiences. How we spend our time is how we spend our lives. Are you happy with your choices?

It's good to check in with ourselves in these areas to stay on track with our beliefs or to shift into greater alignment. It's true that honesty is the best policy! And first we must be honest with ourselves: being true to our word, saying what we do, and doing what we say. We all may have different truths for we are all not playing the same game of life, but most times we know when we've taken a detour into the wilderness versus being in honest territory.

ALL TRUTHS ARE EASY TO UNDERSTAND ONCE THEY ARE DISCOVERED; THE POINT IS TO DISCOVER THEM.

—Galileo Galilei

Have a story to tell, to write, to perform? Ann Randolph encourages students to explore the contradictions within, giving voice to the things that scare us. Through writing and improv workshops and retreats, she uses humor to spotlight truth.
AnnRandolph.com
AnnRandolphKauaiRetreats.com

Time to face the fear of public speaking? Check out a Toastmasters club near you to practice speaking and leadership skills in a supportive environment.
toastmasters.org

A "little white lie" here and there builds up. Keeping stories straight and remembering tall tales is a waste of precious energy. And what is the underlying reason for half-truths anyway . . . hoping to protect another, to save face, to gloss over uncomfortable feelings? It is true that "sometimes the truth hurts" or is scary. But you probably already know the truth on a subconscious level so facing the truth is better in the long run, even if it may cause temporary pain. Get on the fact track, and you probably won't want to turn back.

When we do things out of routine or complacency, we are not mindfully living. Being awake and aware takes energy but once in the flow one receives many more gifts than while asleep at the chakra wheel. Earth doesn't need another cog or drone or sheep. The time to be vibrant, radiant, happy, and healthy is here and now.

If you spend your days in a career that is not in alignment with your ideals, then get proactive in finding a way to shift toward your true calling. What businesses, organizations or activities excite you? Ask, and doors will open. Ask by opening your heart, opening your ears, opening your mouth, and allowing your soul's yearning to come to the surface and breathe.

The throat wants to sing the song of your heart. If the "cat's got your tongue" or you're "all choked up" with a "lump in your throat" emotions and ideas probably want to be expressed. Cry, scream, or cackle! Purge the old in preparation for the new, emptying your bodily vessel so you may renew and begin a fresh journey.

Speak up for yourself, your beliefs, and those unable to speak for themselves. Revolutions and evolutions have been known to occur when people find their voices. It is our duty to discover and speak our truth. If you have something you need to say or create, this is the time for expression. Painters paint, bakers bake, healers heal, dancers dance. How you translate your inner tube of truth is your creative choice. Artistic or other, find clarity and commit to releasing and realizing.

It is well known that public speaking is a huge fear for many. And why wouldn't it be in a world where fear-based, judgmental critics are ever ready to pounce? Choosing not to seek outside validation is a freeing concept. Sure it's nice to be liked, but winning awards, votes, likes or popularity contests is far from the end all be all. It takes courage to put ourselves in front of others with our solid opinions.

If you have ever had a hankering to try stand up comedy, improv, acting, a musical instrument or singing, make today the day you give it a go! Your bathroom mirror is a grand audience to begin with, a music store has guitars to pick at, or make the move to finally sign up for that singing class you've been eyeing.

Open up your blue voice box . . . sing, chant, let your glottis go! Giggle your way through a laughing yoga class. Let sighs and sounds strum your vocal cords. We tone our bodies with weights and asanas, and finding our truth can sometimes be like finding our abs! Requiring discipline, commitment, and positive habits, it's not easy work and nobody can do it for us, but inch by inch we peel back layers to find the muscle of what we are made of.

Now focus the chi/prana/energy coursing through your being by tuning, toning, and honing your magnificent tool with sound vibrations. We are made up of energy, and every molecule in our body responds to sound waves. You probably already have playlists for each occasion from pump-you-up-workouts to sensual-starry-eyed-lovers-unite-by-candlelight-nights.

As above, so below. Usually in the process of conceiving a baby, some sounds are being made. This is also true when the baby is being born. A large amount of tension in the body is held in the jaw, and the jaw relates to the pelvis. The Throat and Sacral areas balance one another hourglass style. When the throat constricts, the birth canal is tight. When the hips are tight, the jaws lock up. Circling the hips and making deep, primal sounds helps in opening the whole body.

YOUR TIME IS LIMITED, SO DON'T WASTE IT LIVING SOMEONE ELSE'S LIFE. DON'T BE TRAPPED BY DOGMA— WHICH IS LIVING WITH THE RESULTS OF OTHER PEOPLE'S THINKING. DON'T LET THE NOISE OF OTHERS' OPINIONS DROWN OUT YOUR OWN INNER VOICE. AND MOST IMPORTANT, HAVE THE COURAGE TO FOLLOW YOUR HEART AND INTUITION. THEY SOMEHOW ALREADY KNOW WHAT YOU TRULY WANT TO BECOME. EVERYTHING ELSE IS SECONDARY.

—Steve Jobs

Try singing a few elongated "OMs" in a row. Feels good, huh? Most all ritual involves music for it is a universal language we feel and vibrate alongside, essentially becoming one with the tunes. Toning helps in unclogging energetic or physical build-ups. Take care to practice good posture and keep a steady breath while toning and chanting. This keeps airways open and energy flowing. We tend to harbor muscular and energetic blockages at our throats. How many teeth grinders are out in the world, stressed out with frequent headache pain? Relax the jaw, mouth, and tongue, and savor letting loose tense temples.

The sound of singing bowls, chimes, bells, tuning forks, a particularly fantastic concert, kirtan, choir or a sea of OMs . . . these awaken our senses and create energizing and/or calming effects that last far beyond the musical set. Our cells become activated and rearrange according to the tunes. Caves, cathedrals, and clubs alike provide echo chambers for sound healing which massage our hearts and minds. Just as joyful euphoria may be unleashed, trauma may be released as well so don't be afraid if tears flow.

Sometimes being silent is the medicine for this day of your cleanse. Many have overactive Throat Chakras that spew, babble and gossip. Unharnessed energy oftentimes manifests in unproductive, often harmful ways. Speak . . . and LISTEN. Explore your voice today, and also be open to listening to life on a deeper level.

Healthy communication of our inner world is a flowing dance of speaking and hearing, giving and receiving, balancing and harmonizing.

STEAMY THROAT COAT AND AROMATIC FACIAL

Deep clean your pores by opening them up with the power of steam. Breathing in a bouquet of herbs submersed in hot water creates a fragrant treat for the senses.

- 3 cups boiling water
- ¼ cup fresh or dried herbs and/or flowers

Use saved herbal teas from the last five days of your cleanse or any herb combination of your choice. Chamomile, tulsi, lemongrass, eucalyptus, and peppermint all work wonderfully in creating a homemade steam room experience. Also, feel free to add a squeezed lemon, a few slices of fresh ginger, or drops of a favorite essential oil to your steamy tea brew.

After boiling water in a saucepan, pour into a bowl that is approximately the size of your face. Add the herbal mixture to the water, allowing it to steep and cool for a few minutes. With a cloth or towel draped over your head, lean over the steaming bowl, making sure the temperature is to your liking Goldilocks style—not too hot, not too cold . . . but just right.

Eyes closed with your cloth cloak creating a sealed environment about a foot away from the water, breathe in the perfumed steam, opening and closing your mouth allowing it to flow through your throat and out your nostrils and vice versa. Dance with your Throat Chakra breath by making sounds and seeing your sound vibrations ripple in the water bowl. Stick out your tongue and release some Lion's breath roars! Rinse your face with cool water, and enjoy smooth skin and breathing.

The quieter you become, the more you can hear.

—Ram Dass

Sanskrit name
Vissudha

Meaning
Purification

Mantra
I SPEAK

Color
blue

Location
throat

Element
vibration

Sense
sound

Areas of Body Influenced
throat, neck, thyroid gland, esophagus, jaws, ears, windpipe, trachea, vocal cords, teeth, tongue, gums, mouth, lips

Meditation
I am a confident communicator, knowing and expressing my truth. Clear in my goals, my internal and external selves are in alignment. I have the right to be heard and speak fluidly from my heart.

Lessons for the Spirit
inner truth, inner child, self-expression, optimism, encouragement, enthusiasm, communication, purity, sincerity, ability to process criticism, capable of receiving information and responding, articulating, releasing, healing

Unbalanced
lying, gossiping, bragging, manipulating, weak voice, harsh voice, shyness, overly talkative, sore throat, dental issues, hearing problems, tightness in jaws, teeth grinding, thyroid dysfunction, difficulty in creatively expressing oneself

Balancing Activities
singing, chanting, laughing, screaming, speaking, listening, understanding, toasting, confessing, storytelling, sharing thoughts, listening to music, making music, toning, writing, ujjayi breathing, shoulder stands, surrounding yourself with the color BLUE

Vibrational Sound
EE (long E)

Seed Sound
HAM

Tonal Key
G

Gems, Crystals, and Minerals
aquamarine, turquoise, blue lace agate, azurite, celestite, amazonite, chrysocolla, chalcedony, lapis lazuli

Essential Oils
eucalyptus, sage, lemongrass, lemon, slippery elm, trumpet vine, thyme, bergamot, licorice, horehound, balsam fir

ChakWave Herbal Blend
red clover blossoms, blue vervain flower, nettles

THE THROAT CHAKRA: YOGA POSTURES

Matsyasana
(Fish Pose)

Halasana
(Plow Pose)

Purvottanasana
(Upward Plank Pose)

Salamba Sarvangasana
(Supported Shoulderstand)

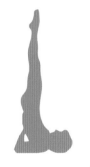

Ustrasana
(Camel Pose)

THE THROAT CHAKRA: RECIPE

Ingredients

2 cups blueberries
one bunch celery (around 10 stalks)
one lemon
½ cup ChakWave herbal tea (optional)
2 teaspoons chia seeds (optional)

Directions

Brew the herbal tea and allow to cool while juicing
the celery (chop off white end so ribs can be washed
thoroughly) and lemon (peel first). Place juiced celery
and lemon in blender, and add the whole blueberries. The
blueberry peels are utilized in this recipe yielding an extra
nutritional punch plus the blue hue. Mix in herbal tea and
whisk with chia seeds.

If you prefer less sweetness, you may choose to juice
just the celery. If you opt for this all veggie version, it won't
be blue. Drinking only water and/or herbal tea today is also
an option.

THE THROAT CHAKRA: NUTRITION

Anthocyanin antioxidants strengthen the cardiovascular system and provide the pigment that puts the "blue" in BLUEBERRIES. Native Americans believed these berries with a five-pointed star blossom were sent from the Great Spirit to alleviate hunger in the children. Indigenous peoples drank blueberry juice medicinally to ease coughs and also taught the English Pilgrim settlers how to farm, gather, and store them.

Gracefully long like a neck, CELERY lowers blood pressure, alkalizes the body by balancing acidity, and contains acetylenics, which inhibit the growth of cancerous tumors. While the magnesium in these crunchy, throat-y stalks helps calm the nervous system, celery's pheromones work overtime to boost the libido! Garlands of celery have adorned the dead from ancient Greece to Pharaoh Tutankhamun.

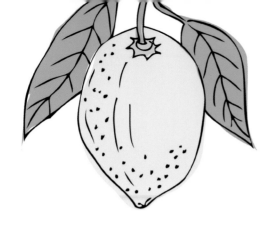

When life gives you **LEMONS**...juice them! Alkalizing lemons are at the top of most health-conscious grocery lists. Filled with immune boosting Vitamin C, lemons target tonsillitis, sore throats, runny noses, and coughs. Antibacterial and antiviral, lemon juice can be dabbed onto pimples, fever blisters, and bug bites to help speed the healing process. Toxin flushing lemons are also breath freshening and skin softening.

A phlegm loosening expectorant, **RED CLOVER BLOSSOM** heals coughs and respiratory issues. The three oval leaves have been associated with the Celtic Triple Goddess (maiden, mother, crone) as well as the Christian Trinity (father, son, holy ghost). Sip red clover blossom tea to reduce plaque build up in arteries, purify blood, and lessen menopausal symptoms like hot flashes. A member of the legume family, these blossoms, when planted in tired pastures, enrich and rejuvenate soil while also adding nitrogen.

NETTLES stimulate lymphatic cleansing and fortify the endocrine system by boosting thyroid health. The leaves relieve allergies and reduce inflammation in the urinary tract and prostate. Tibetan yogi Jetsun Milarepa is said to have lived for years only on nettle tea while meditating and teaching and is often depicted in sculptures and paintings with green hued skin.

Coughs, colds, and respiratory ailments ranging from shortness of breath to wheezing gasps head for the hills when *BLUE VERVAIN FLOWER* enters the system. Vervain is derived from the Celtic word "ferfaen" meaning "to drive away" as the Druids believed this medicinal herb scared off menacing spirits while calling in creative inspiration. In Egyptian mythology the flowers originated as tears of the fertility goddess Isis. Christians named blue vervain the "herb of the cross" as it is said to be the compress applied to Jesus's wounds when crucified. Native Americans revere it as a sacred medicine and grind the buds into flour for baking.

THE THROAT CHAKRA: JOURNAL PROMPT

I SPEAK . . .

Writing with your non-dominant hand, channel your inner child with scribbly markings.

_____

_____

_____

_____

What messages does the kid within have for you? Look up into the blue sky and remember what the pure voice said before others told you what to think or how to act. What did you love to do as a child? When playing dress up and make believe, what would you become . . . a singer, doctor, farmer, actor, entrepreneur, teacher, parent? These pure childhood dream impulses give us good insight into discovering our truest callings.

_____

_____

_____

_____

_____

If you find yourself beaten down or in a bind, ask how you got there. Can you name the beliefs that tend to bring you down? Do these beliefs lead to some destructive behaviors or bad habits? Where did these thoughts form? Whose voice is in your head? Is it a parent, friend, teacher, or leader? Take the time to discover who is unconsciously telling you what to do or what your values and morals *should* be. Thank them for their time and contribution to your life and growth. Now step away, bid them farewell and welcome *your* freedom of expression.

_____

_____

_____

_____

_____

What do you have to say?

_____

_____

_____

_____

_____

You've got to keep the child alive; you can't create without it.

—Joni Mitchell

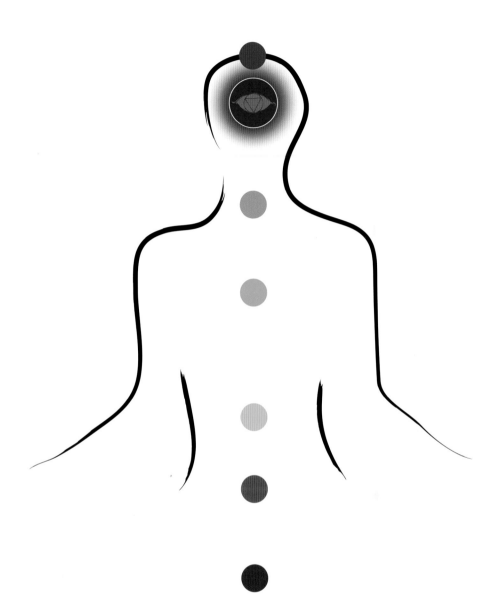

"I SEE"

Day 6

THE THIRD EYE
CHAKRA

THE THIRD EYE CHAKRA
ENCOURAGES INTUITION,
IMAGINATION, DREAMS,
AND VISION. AS THE
MIND'S EYE, IT IS OUR
LIGHT AND TELEPATHIC
POWER POINT.

AS YOU DRINK YOUR THIRD EYE TONIC, dream big today and let your insightful "sixth sense" kick in to illuminate life! When honoring inner sight, we unlock the potential to see the light. Ever have an inkling, idea, premonition, hunch, or vibe? By trusting both intelligence and intuition, awareness becomes finely tuned. We are more able to follow the spiritual breadcrumbs along our paths.

Signs and symbolism begin to make sense and have greater, applicable meaning in our lives. If one isn't in tune with their Third Eye capabilities, they probably don't give much credence to anything they cannot see with their physical eyes. Acknowledging and activating intuition raises your frequency to where you can better tap into the collective consciousness and ancient wisdom.

The concept of the Third Eye is found in many cultures. Many people in Asia and beyond wear Bindis, dots of paint or stickers on the forehead between the eyes, to encourage concentration and positive thoughts as well as remind them of their innate Third Eye wisdom. In the Catholic tradition, ash is used to mark the forehead on Ash Wednesday in a ceremony of remembering Christ Consciousness. From ancient Egyptians revering the Eye of Horus symbol for protection to Hinduism's Shiva burning through untruths with his third eye, this power point is present.

EVERY GREAT DREAM BEGINS WITH A DREAMER. ALWAYS REMEMBER, YOU HAVE WITHIN YOU THE STRENGTH, THE PATIENCE, AND THE PASSION TO REACH FOR THE STARS TO CHANGE THE WORLD.

—*Harriet Tubman*

In the physical body, the pineal gland is associated with the Third Eye, and it actually looks like a small pinecone shaped eye. Located in the center of the brain, the pineal and pituitary glands are the only structures in the brain not bilaterally symmetrical or members of a pair. Scientists have found the pineal gland produces hormones as well as serotonin and melatonin, which regulate everything from the cycles of waking and sleeping to happiness. But this little gland that could goes much deeper as 16th century French philosopher René Descartes called it "the seat of the soul" and Greek anatomist Herophilus spoke of it as "a sphincter which regulates the flow of thought." It holds the mystique of being the connector between the physical, mental, and spiritual realms and perhaps even a telepathic portal into other spheres.

AUM.
ASATO MA SAD-GAMAYA;
TAMASO MA JYOTIR-GAMAYA;
MRTYOR-MA AMRUTAM GAMAYA.
AUM. SHANTI, SHANTI SHANTI.
(AUM. LEAD ME FROM UNREAL TO REAL;
LEAD ME FROM DARKNESS TO LIGHT;
LEAD ME FROM DEATH TO IMMORTALITY.
AUM . . . PEACE, PEACE, PEACE.)

— *Brihadaranyaka Upanishad 1.3.28*

TAKE A MOMENT TO EXERCISE ALL THREE EYES. Look up and down, side to side, and make circles clockwise and counter clockwise. Do each ten times. These eye asanas help to increase blood flow to the brain improving memory and assisting the synapses in synapsing!

Now rub your palms together to generate warmth. Cupping your hands over closed eyes, make yourself some funky bubble goggles and allow the physical eyes to rest while honing your third eye of perception. In yogic practices, this drawing inward of the senses is called Pratyahara. With one pinky finger gently massage the sensitive third eye spot on your forehead, quieting your mind and pleasantly hanging out in the ethers for a while.

Focus on focusing by concentrating on a drishti, or focal point. This may be any spot around you, as long as it is stationary. A notch on the floor, mark on the wall, top of a mountain, or the tip of your nose all work. The goal is to keep the mind as stable and still as the point of your choice. As the world at large can be overstimulating, gazing at a candle with limited blinks is a useful technique for softening first the visual distractions and in time the internal ones. Mandalas are also very useful for harnessing attention via geometrical designs symbolizing everything from purpose to peace, creativity to consciousness. They are visual representations of order on the outside which help in creating order within.

As you softly gaze, let your self, thoughts, and imagination prance the spiraling pathways toward inner guidance and wholeness where all is connected. The joy or suffering of your neighbor or a being on the other side of the planet is your joy and suffering as well. Embrace the web of connectivity, see the world in a different light, from a supernatural point of view where everything is energy, and people are playing their karmic roles. This helps in the process of forgiving yourself and others. Being mindful without judging, acceptance is your go to. Once you've observed inwardly, take it outside and be an aware observer of the world.

Sit on a park bench and settle in for some people watching. Check out the body language of persons strolling solo, hanging with their pets, babies, friends, or lovers. Notice stances, cadences, and chemistries. In your mind's eye, complete their stories. Where are they from, what is their relationship, what are their dreams? Filling in the blanks helps hone the intuitive third eye muscle . . . not to mention making for a fun afternoon.

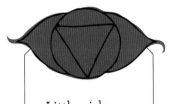

Little girls
with dreams
become women
with vision.

—Unknown

WE'RE NOT HERE TO COMPARE OURSELVES TO OTHER PEOPLE, BUT TO COMPARE OUR ACTIONS TO OUR DREAMS.

—Dr. John Demartini

Instinctually we know much more than we are usually willing to give ourselves credit for. Impulses are many times brushed aside as impractical. The next time you don't have solid proof of something but get a funny feeling, allow yourself to be aware of it. Maybe you immediately listen to and heed your instinct or at least write it down to circle back round on your hunch. Treat the muscle of instinct like you would your biceps by doing push-ups. A few per day add up and build your intuitive strength.

IMAGINATION IS EVERYTHING.
IT IS THE PREVIEW OF LIFE'S
COMING ATTRACTIONS.

—*Albert Einstein*

Many may want to shun, lock up, demonize, or write off persons whom have accessed some level of the Third Eye Chakra as delusional or crazy. Visions and mystical or religious experiences open new routes in a system, and the ability and willingness to pull back the curtain, to see beyond the veil, needs to be nurtured and supported in order to have a fluid growth experience. Cleansing and refining the body helps in healthily reaching higher mental and spiritual energies inviting consciousness to ascend. We must leave behind our comfort zones in order to chase dreams. Whether frightened of success, having difficulty making decisions, or experiencing a lack of imagination, help appears when you are open to it. Set aside time to fantasize and daydream, visualizing in order to manifest. Using your imagination, see yourself living your dreams. What does it look and feel like? Where are you, who are you with, what are you doing? Feel into it. By doing this you are setting the scene for yourself to move into living that life in the physical realm. Explore the limitless possibilities.

ONCE YOU REPLACE NEGATIVE
THOUGHTS WITH POSITIVE
ONES, YOU'LL START HAVING
POSITIVE RESULTS.

—*Willie Nelson*

*Go confidently in
the direction of your
dreams. Live the life
you've imagined.*

—Henry David Thoreau

Without grounding and gumption, dreams are illusions. While in pursuit of yours, you must still pay rent and buy groceries. In the "in between time" of aligning dreams with waking life, make the absolute best of the "mundane" tasks, jobs, and commitments by looking at them as a "chop wood, carry water" meditation. Stay present and let "little" successes keep morale afloat. While we may have "cup half empty" days and feel discouraged, stay constantly amazed by your capabilities of persistence and tenacity.

Gain knowledge in whatever it is that interests you . . . culinary arts, acting, hula hooping, painting, scuba diving, piano, [fill in the blank with your love]. Boost your mind and mind's eye educating yourself via books, films, travel, striking up conversations with strangers, and surrounding yourself with positive and present goal-oriented individuals. Be diligent in studies and confident in progress, holding on to your dreams while acknowledging they are constantly evolving and the Universe is conspiring to help you.

YOU ARE NEVER TOO OLD
TO SET ANOTHER GOAL OR
TO DREAM A NEW DREAM.

—*C.S. Lewis*

This little light of mine, I'm gonna let it shine.

This little light of mine, I'm gonna let it shine,

let it shine, let it shine, let it shine.

Hide it under a bushel, no. I'm gonna let it shine.

Hide it under a bushel, no.

I'm gonna let it shine, let it shine, let it shine, let it shine.

—Harry Dixon Loes

Sanskrit name
Ajna

Meaning
Command Center

Mantra
I SEE

Color
indigo

Location
center of forehead

Element
ether

Sense
intuition

Areas of Body Influenced
eyes, brain, brow, pineal gland, forehead, cerebellum, sinuses

Meditation
Honoring my inner sight and wisdom, I am intuitive and imaginative. Psychically attuned to my inspired pathway, I have the capacity to see and heal.

Lessons for the Spirit
clarity, imagination, freedom from illusion, intuition, concentration, visualization, psychic abilities, premonitions, extrasensory perception (ESP), capacity to make sense of symbolism, awareness of auras and spirit guides, telepathy, clairvoyance, precognition, shamanic abilities

Unbalanced
paranoia, worry, manipulation, hysteria, depression, hallucinations, issues with vision and sinuses, headaches, stress, irritability, nightmares, panic attacks, shock, inability to distinguish between fantasy and reality, over analysis, overly sensitive toward what others think and feel, poor memory, lack of clarity and focus

Balancing Activities
visualization exercises, gazing at mandalas, practical application of psychic insights and instincts, craniosacral and myofacial treatments, hypnotherapy, speaking with a psychiatrist, energy work, psychedelic experiences, surrounding yourself with the color INDIGO

Vibrational Sound
MmmNnn

Seed Sound
AUM

Tonal Key
A

Gems, Crystals, and Minerals
moonstone, sapphire, sodalite, fluorite, iolite, labradorite, tanzanite, snowflake obsidian, kyanite

Essential Oils
mint, jasmine, mugwort, saffron, star anise, geranium, helichrysum, gardenia

ChakWave herbal blend
eyebright leaf, ginkgo biloba leaf, amla berry

THE THIRD EYE CHAKRA: YOGA POSTURES

Garudasana
(Eagle Pose)

Makarasana
(Dolphin Pose)

Balasana
(Child's Pose)

Vajrasana
(Thunderbolt Pose)

Bakasana
(Crow Pose)

THE THIRD EYE CHAKRA: RECIPE

Ingredients

3 grapefruits
3 pomegranates (around 3 cups seeds)
2 heaping cups blackberries
½ cup ChakWave herbal tea (optional)

Directions

Brew herbal tea and allow to cool.

Remove the pomegranate seeds (arils) from the white membrane. An effective way to approach this is by filling a bowl with water and submersing a quartered pomegranate. As your nimble fingers pluck out the little rubies, the membrane floats to the top of the water and can be easily removed and placed into the compost bin. Seeds can also be purchased fresh or frozen and already freed. Juice the pomegranate seeds.

Peel the grapefruits, and juice in your juicing machine or with a citrus juicer.

You have a choice as to how to proceed with the blackberries. You may juice or blend them. If you juice, you may want to put any moist pulp through your juicer again so as to get all the juicy goodness out of these soft berries. If you blend, add the pomegranate and grapefruit juices to the blender as well. Use your intuition to guide you on whether to blend or to juice! :)

Mix all of the juices and tea together. Chia seeds are optional today as the blackberries provide a similarly seedy crunch factor.

You may also choose to drink only water and/or herbal tea today.

THE THIRD EYE CHAKRA: NUTRITION

Packed with polyphenols and potassium, every part of the **POMEGRANATE** plant (root, bark, flowers, fruit, leaves) is used for medicinal purposes in Ayurveda right down to the last dropper full of sweet/tart juice to treat cataracts! These tiny seeds are the cornerstone of the origin myth of the seasons as Persephone ate a few given to her by Hades and then had to split her time between his wintery underworld and Earth's spring surface with her mom Demeter.

Dark blue and filled with a slew of antioxidants, **BLACKBERRIES** are anti-bacterial and anti-viral. These multi-seeded, bioflavenoid filled berries are used for everything from curing gout and anemia to settling stomachs and lifting spirits. The thorny briars were once planted for protection around graves to keep robbers at bay as well as the dead from rising as ghosts.

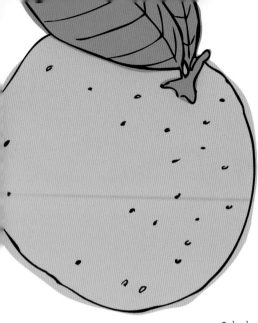

A hybrid of pomelos and sweet oranges, **GRAPEFRUITS** were originally called the "forbidden fruit" in Barbados. In 1814, the name grapefruit came along in Jamaica based on their grape-like clusters. These sweet and sour Vitamin C and lycopene packed gems lower cholesterol and repair DNA. They contain Vitamin A and beta carotene which decrease macular degeneration improving eye health.

EYEBRIGHT for eyesight . . . the name says it all! For a bright-eyed future, ingest or use as a compress to help heal pinkeye, cataracts, styes, and weeping allergy eyes. A few centuries ago, pub people were sipping Eyebright Ale and dripping feathers wet with eyebright tea into their eyes for clearer vision. While strengthening strained eyes, this mighty herb also strengthens a weak memory.

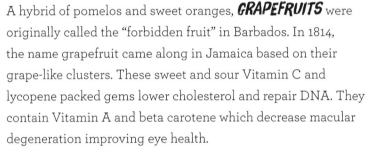

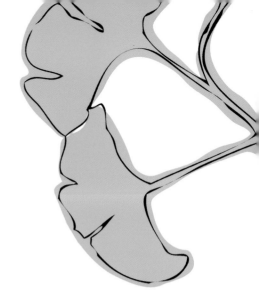

Brain cell nourishing **GINKGO BILOBA** leaf increases blood flow to the brain, boosting energy and increasing the ability to concentrate. Ginkgo has been used to prevent and treat depression, vertigo, strokes, and ringing ears. Around during our dinosaur era, the tough ginkgo biloba tree is the oldest tree on the planet and has been dubbed a "living fossil."

The **AMLA BERRY** is a longevity-inducing, anti-aging Ayurvedic superstar. Divine lovers Krishna and Radha are said to have lived in an amalaki tree amongst the berries. These berries carry carotene which enhances eyes freeing one from cataracts, night blindness, and intraocular pressure. A dosha balancer, amla is used to cure everything from high blood pressure to bronchitis, diarrhea to diabetes.

THE THiRD EYE CHAKRA: JOuRNAL PROMPT

I SEE . . .

Draw your dreams. Grab some colored pencils, throw planning and judging out the window, and enjoy some imagination stimulating improv art making! Settle your mind, clear blockages so the cosmos may meet the earth, and let images and words flow freely. No need to be stingy with ideas. When plugged into the universe, they are infinite.

_____

_____

_____

_____

_____

Ask a direct question in your illustrated note, and literally put the paper beneath your pillow. Set the prayerful intention you would appreciate guidance, direction, and inspiration. Make the conscious decision to dream on it, and be open to receiving messages.

_____

_____

_____

_____

_____

Go to bed, and welcome vivid visuals. When sleeping, pay attention to all images or feelings. Be open to getting up in the middle of the night if you need to take notes, and immediately upon waking, write down any musings or messages. Sweet dreams.

_____

_____

_____

_____

_____

There are some people
who live in a dream
world, and some who face
reality; and then there
are those who turn one
into the other.

—Douglas Everett

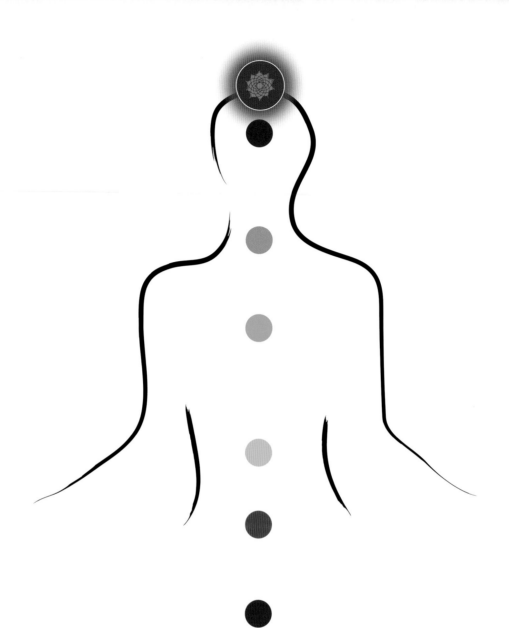

"I KNOW"

Day 7

THE CROWN
CHAKRA

THE CROWN CHAKRA CONNECTS US WITH THE COSMIC CONSCIOUSNESS OF THE UNIVERSE AND IS ALIGNED WITH AWARENESS, WISDOM, AND BLISS. THIS IS THE SPACE OF SACRED ENLIGHTENMENT.

TIME TO BLOSSOM! The thousand petaled lotus flower springs from the swampy mud. With deep roots anchoring and supporting a healthy system, the flower of life unfolds releasing the sweet nectar of knowing and Crown Chakra bliss.

Moving from innocence into wisdom may be challenging at times, but there are infinite rewards for taking the leap. Opening up our channels, pathways, and perceptions to higher consciousness and finding our unity with the divine ... is divine!

The entire universe is within you. That's a big concept to wrap a brain around ... and that's because it's probably next to impossible to do so. We must go beyond our brains and minds into the realm of the universal. Big picture, Godhead stuff here. Glowing halos are present in many artistic interpretations of awareness and spiritual enlightenment. Christ, Buddha, and Saints are adorned with these divine energy light auras above the head.

You are amazingly magical and remind the rest of us we are as well! Be in awe of yourself and others. You, yes YOU, are whole and capable of accessing the treasure of awakening. Glow and be a lighthouse...a beacon of hope, grace, and joy. So many times we block ourselves from expansive freedom and peace because we're telling the same worn out story to ourselves and others.

THE SOUL SHOULD ALWAYS STAND AJAR, READY TO WELCOME THE ECSTATIC EXPERIENCE.

—*Emily Dickinson*

Everyone deserves a chance at freedom, and we must release in order to be free. Give yourself permission to wonder and wander aim-fully. Your soul sees the aerial view, not the seemingly treacherous mountain passes. Take part in activities that bring you pleasure and increase your vibration as well as facing the darkness. How can you shine light for the impoverished, the prisoners, the oppressed, the corrupt, and those caught in the cycle of conflict?

When we become accustomed to being plugged into our pure power source we become fearless. It takes strength to rise above the petty, to remove all labels and dissolve made-up boundaries between people, beliefs, and dimensions. They get in the way of what truly IS, clouding our minds with chatter, noise, and judgment. Yogis call this state of blessed and blissed oneness Samadhi.

Spend some quality solo time today and enjoy the recalibrating stillness. Give yourself time to transition from the chaos into a meditative place of receiving. Create a space where you will not be interrupted or disturbed. You may choose to sit on a pillow, block, chair, or the ground. Turn off all electronics and things that beep. Close the door, draw the curtains.

Consider creating an altar space for sacred objects meaningful to you. This may include photos, notes, affirmations, books, cards, incense, a singing bowl, a rich tapestry, candles, herbs, a smudge stick, fresh fruit, or flowers. Every sacred space is unique and individual.

Feel like some music? Listen to something instrumental without words or perhaps a guided meditation to help you settle and calm. You may want to do some breathing exercises before meditation to move energy, wake up, or relax.

In a comfortable seated position (which may be different for every body) balance yourself and utilize the power of posture by rolling your shoulders back so your shoulder blades are leaning in together for a kiss and your heart is open. Hold your head high, and keep your chin up . . . literally! Straighten your back. Let your hands rest on your knees, palms facing up in order to energetically receive and release.

Let your past and future, worries and doubts, rest in a little sleeping bag perched on a shelf in your brain. Acknowledge thoughts like a cloud in the sky, seeing them drift pass. Now . . . "be here now." Go inward and open to your higher self and the divine, allowing messages, resolutions, and peace to enter. You are meditation. You ARE home, and you are OM.

Visualize a French press sieving your body from the top of your head down through your toes. This screen with tiny holes pushes down any impurities in your being, any dark matter lurking is slowly compressed through the chakras all the way down to your legs, ankles, and finally out the soles of your feet where we send the muck into the earth to be transmuted and purified. Soul to Sole.

Gracefully gather up the vibrating energy of the sacred and raise your arms wide overhead. Let your hands meet thumb-by-thumb, pinky-by-pinky, forming a lotus cup. Visualize a channel of powerful, pulsating energy emanating from the heavens down your spine, winding through ligaments, tendons, knees, and toes. Let this column of light flow and circle through you from crown to ground and back again.

Now that you've consumed the colors of the rainbow in juice form, consciously breathe them in. Visualize all the air surrounding you as violet. Deeply inhale and allow the color to permeate your being, bathing you with cleansing light. Stay present breathing in this color until you feel the process is complete, and then exhale fully.

Vedic knowledge texts tell of ancient Rishis (seers) partaking in sacred ceremonies where the medicinal plant beverage soma was consumed. No one knows exactly what the concoction was, but during these revelatory rituals they often experienced visions and transcendence. The channeled information was then discussed and written down in hymns and chants. Since the beginning of human history people have reverently worked with flora and fungi modalities to heal and reveal. "Soma-esque" mind altering and expanding plant medicines include (and are certainly not limited to) cannabis sativa (marijuana), psilocybin mushrooms, mescaline, salvia divinorum, peyote, and ayahuasca.

Work your way down through the colors of the rainbow . . . indigo, blue, green, yellow, orange, and red. When finished working with red, ground the entire color spectrum through the soles of your feet. Feel the rainbow flowing through you from head to toe.

Take the meditation mindset with you when walking, skateboarding, washing the dishes, hugging trees, or whatever it is that keeps you in the place of connection with universal consciousness. When you're in the sweet spot of communing with spirit you can be sitting on a pillow, plane, or motorcycle. Be your own Yoda.

Hit up a playground and hang upside down on monkey bars. They're not just for kids! Do a cartwheel, or fold your body over while sitting or standing. Turning your crown upside down not only allows you a view from a different POV, but all the oxygen rich blood circulating through your beautiful brain is a tonic for improving memory and creating healthy, glowing skin. Have fun, laugh, and take chances. Things on Earth don't always happen according to the timeline devised in our minds, but we do seem to get the information we need when we are ready to receive it. As we keep releasing the egos, stepping outside our comfort zones, and following spiritual messages towards what truly turns us on, interests from yesteryear begin to resurface, wisdom comes forward, and connections come full circle.

When you open your life up to trust the unfolding of the lotus blossom, you send the signal that you are receptive and open to the space where anything is possible. The Crown Chakra is infinite, transcendent, and invites us to elevate our spirits, exploring consciousness and our place in time and space.

KEEP AWAY FROM PEOPLE WHO TRY TO BELITTLE YOUR AMBITIONS. SMALL PEOPLE ALWAYS DO THAT, BUT THE REALLY GREAT MAKE YOU FEEL THAT YOU, TOO, CAN BECOME GREAT.

—*Mark Twain*

True enlightenment is nothing but the nature of one's own self being fully realized.

—Dalai Lama

Sanskrit name
Sahasrara

Meaning
Thousand Petaled Lotus

Mantra
I KNOW

Color
violet (and white)

Location
crown of head

Element
space

Sense
spirit

Areas of Body Influenced
brain, pituitary gland, cerebrum, cerebral cortex, central nervous system

Meditation
One with my higher self, all beings, and the divine, I am united with all that is, ever has been, and ever will be. I am unlimited and infinite.

Lessons for the Spirit
alignment with your highest self, existence, and the Universe, pure being, peace, bliss, wisdom, spirituality, consciousness, enlightenment, devotion, inspiration, energy, pure potential, freedom from ego and pride, self awareness and realization, vibration as a manifestation of Source, ability to see the self in others, free of blocks and negativity, ability to transform

Unbalanced
confusion, stress, superstitious, lack of purpose, self-limiting beliefs, frustration, destructive, indecisiveness, apathetic, inability to understand and retain knowledge, headaches, unsure and unclear mind, worry, anxiety, mental and cognitive problems, taking things personally

Balancing Activities
meditating, being in silence, fasting, prayer, inversions, Vipassana, ritual, napping, paying attention, bending forward and hanging head, headstands, examining one's belief system, strategic thinking and planning, lighting incense, plant medicines, connecting with your highest self and Source, surrounding yourself with the colors VIOLET and WHITE

Vibrational Sound
NgNg (ying ying)

Seed Sound
OM

Tonal Key
B

Gems, Crystals, and Minerals
amethyst, diamond, quartz, white opal, white calcite, white topaz, iolate, sugilite, apophyllite, purple fluorite, rainbow moonstone

Essential Oils
sandalwood, frankincense, palo santo, neroli, galbanum, Nag Champa, spikenard, ylang-ylang, nutmeg, valerian

ChakWave herbal blend
lavender flowers, lotus stamens, gotu kola leaf

THE CROWN CHAKRA: YOGA POSTURES

Salamba Sirsasana
(Supported Headstand)

Padmasana
(Lotus Pose)

Prasarita Padottanasana
(Wide-Legged Forward Bend)

Viparita Karani
(Legs-Up-The-Wall Pose)

Savasana
(Corpse Pose)

THE CROWN CHAKRA: RECIPE

Ingredients

1 personal sized watermelon

2 cups red grapes

½ cup ChakWave herbal blend (optional)

Directions

The Crown Chakra recipe is a deliciously light, sweet, and hydrating combination. Enjoy this "dessert day" of the cleanse . . . you've earned it!

Brew herbal tea and allow to cool. Thoroughly wash the watermelon rind and slice the entire melon (rind, white, green, pink, and seeds) into strips that fit your juicer.

Juice the watermelon. Wash the grapes (stalk and all) and feed them through your juicer. Mix together juices and tea, and whisk in chia seeds.

You may also choose to drink only water and/or herbal tea today.

THE CROWN CHAKRA: NUTRITION

Flavorful and refreshing **WATERMELONS** supply a Vitamin B6 brain boost, are low calorie, and may even hinder fat storage in cells. Electrolytes keep you hydrated, and amino acids citrulline and arginine get the blood flowing. Literally about the size of a person's head, the seeds within these watery melons are nicely symbolic of the powerful potential seeded in each of us. In the pink, potassium and lycopene work to protect skin from sun damamge and reduce wrinkles while the green rind provides chlorophyl.

Like the weaving Kundalini energy of the chakra system, **RED GRAPES** grow upwards toward the sky as a vine. They contain phenols which help protect and assist neurons in the brain. Resveratrol not only helps blood vessel walls keep elasticity, but this compound also helps in preserving memory and heightening mood.

A gorgeous violet color, soothing **LAVENDER FLOWER** has a physically and emotionally calming effect which can alleviate anxiety, tension, and depression. Decreasing stress and insomnia, the aromatic and relaxing flowers help with sleeping and healing. Romans used this purple gem in perfuming baths, and the name lavender comes from the Latin "lavare" which means "to wash."

Clearing the sinuses and opening the respiratory system, **LOTUS STAMENS** move stagnant energy and promote pleasantly heightened perception. Symbolic of non-attachment and spiritual awakening, lotus brings relaxation, tranquility, and lifts moods by boosting serotonin production.

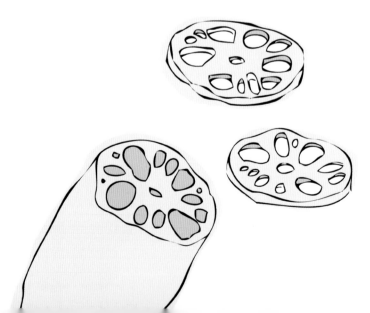

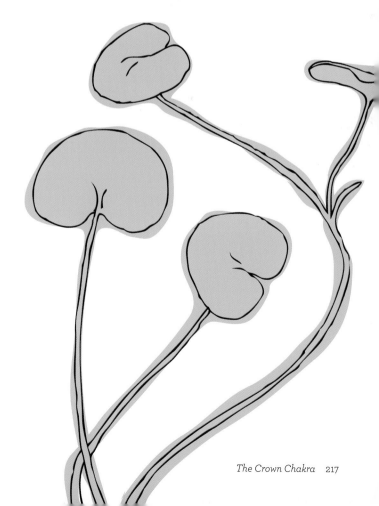

GOTU KOLA enhances blood flow to the brain and body which is helpful in enhancing memory and concentration as well as putting the kibosh on varicose veins and bruises. This hormone balancing adaptogen has been dubbed "the secret of perpetual youth" and is said to promote wisdom and clarity of consciousness.

THE CROWN CHAKRA: JOURNAL PROMPT

I KNOW . . .

Who are you? What do you believe in and stand for? What are your feelings about living and dying? What is your understanding of the universe, oneness, and the divine mystery that holds us all?

_____

_____

_____

_____

_____

_____

_____

_____

_____

_____

_____

_____

_____

_____

_____

_____

_____

_____

_____

_____

_____

When (if ever) have you felt connected to everything and everyone? How do you plan to hang out in that space more often? As waves fold back into the ocean from where they came, the Crown Chakra of enlightenment becomes one with the infinite ocean of consciousness. Are you an evolutionary activist? How can you help in raising the consciousness of all?

_____

_____

_____

_____

_____

_____

_____

_____

_____

_____

_____

_____

_____

_____

_____

_____

_____

_____

_____

_____

USE THE WATERMELON AND GRAPE PULP

(or any leftover vegetables or fruits you may have from your week of cleansing) to create an amazing facial for your skin. Now that you are glowing from within, let the fresh produce work its beautiful magic on the outside as well.

Carrots, cucumbers, cantaloupe . . . clean out the crisper so that nothing goes to waste! Juice the rainbow of produce, drink up, and apply the pulp to a clean face or better yet hop in the shower to douse yourself with the whole batch for firm, toned skin to round out your cleanse week and have some juices to drink post cleanse.

OUR DEEPEST FEAR IS NOT THAT WE
ARE INADEQUATE. OUR DEEPEST FEAR
IS THAT WE ARE POWERFUL BEYOND
MEASURE. IT IS OUR LIGHT, NOT OUR
DARKNESS THAT MOST FRIGHTENS US.

WE ASK OURSELVES, WHO AM I
TO BE BRILLIANT, GORGEOUS,
TALENTED, FABULOUS?

ACTUALLY, WHO ARE YOU NOT TO BE?
YOU ARE A CHILD OF GOD. YOUR PLAYING
SMALL DOES NOT SERVE THE WORLD.
THERE IS NOTHING ENLIGHTENED ABOUT
SHRINKING SO THAT OTHER PEOPLE WON'T
FEEL INSECURE AROUND YOU. WE ARE
ALL MEANT TO SHINE, AS CHILDREN DO.

WE WERE BORN TO MAKE MANIFEST
THE GLORY OF GOD THAT IS WITHIN US.
IT'S NOT JUST IN SOME OF US; IT'S IN
EVERYONE. AND AS WE LET OUR OWN
LIGHT SHINE, WE UNCONSCIOUSLY
GIVE OTHER PEOPLE PERMISSION TO
DO THE SAME. AS WE ARE LIBERATED
FROM OUR OWN FEAR, OUR PRESENCE
AUTOMATICALLY LIBERATES OTHERS.

—*Marianne Williamson*

Part V

BEYOND THE CLEANSE

And the end of all our exploring will be to arrive where we started and know the place for the first time.

—T.S. Eliot

IT'S TIME TO EAT AGAIN. Be gentle with yourself. Begin with raw foods, simple soups, and salads. For culinary inspiration, revisit the sample three day, plant based menu on page 32 that eased you into the cleanse. You may want to take some time to connect with other ChakWave cleansers online as sharing your experience with others transforming and healing is powerful. The pathway and plan come together as we join forces.

When you have completed the ChakWave cleanse, chances are you will enjoy increased awareness of your body—how you operate, what goes in, and what comes out. You will have hands-on experience with healthy vegetables, fruits, herbs, spices and the ChakWave juice recipes in your culinary repertoire.

CHAKRALYN RECOMMENDS . . . SUPER SALADS!

Superfood and super delicious. Create a masterpiece with the darkest leafy greens you can find . . . kale, arugula, and spinach are great options. Cut up a combo of cabbage, cauliflower, Brussels sprouts, broccoli, and/or carrots.

For crunch factor, get nutty! Walnuts, almonds, pecans, or cashews are perfect. Fresh or dried fruit like cranberries, strawberries, or apricots gives delicious flavor bursts and beautiful color. Dress with your unique blend of vinegar, olive oil, pomegranate, orange, or lemon juice, mustard, salt, pepper, or freshly chopped herbs.

LOVE YOURSELF
FIRST, AND
EVERYTHING
ELSE FALLS
INTO LINE.
YOU REALLY
HAVE TO LOVE
YOURSELF TO
GET ANYTHING
DONE IN THIS
WORLD.

—*Lucille Ball*

Deeper chakra system knowledge is added to your conscious living arsenal. After completing this cleanse you may experience a major sense of accomplishment that promises to multiply into other realms of your life. When you set an intention, stick to it and learn from it, the possibilities are limitless. Now let your clear mind, healthy body, and newfound energy propel you into your amazing future!

RECOMMENDED TOOLS FOR FURTHER KNOWLEDGE:

Eastern Body, Western Mind: Psychology and the Chakra System as a Path to the Self by Anodea Judith, PhD

Chakra Foods for Optimum Health: A Guide to the Foods that can Improve Your Energy, Inspire Creative Changes, Open Your Heart, and Heal Body, Mind, and Spirit by Deanna Minich, PhD

Anatomy of the Spirit: The Seven Stages of Power and Healing by Caroline Myss, PhD

Aroma Yoga: A Guide for Using Essential Oils in Your Yoga Practice by Tracy Griffiths and Ashley Turner

Sacred Mirrors: The Visionary Art of Alex Grey by Alex Grey with Ken Wilber and Carlo McCormick

Chakra Beats music by Andrea Brook and William Close

Use your life to serve
the world, and you
will find that it also
serves you.

—Oprah Winfrey

ACKNOWLEDGMENTS

I give thanks for my family: my parents Carol and Tom Richey, my grandmothers Eileen Rhoades and Ogoretta Richey, my aunt Jan Richey and uncle Tom Lamphere. They formed a steadfast foundation from which I was able to build my life. Many thanks to my brother Emory and sister-in-law Stephanie Richey and friends Liz Leknickas, Panos Stoumpos, and Danielle Sternlicht for helping me pound the pavement sampling juices and connecting with the ChakWave community at festivals and neighborhood shops.

I have learned much from my teachers: Lalit Kumar of Himalaya Yoga Valley in Goa, India; the amazing books, chakra psychology, and chakra yoga classes of Sacred Centers founder Anodea Judith in Northern California, Chef Eric Crowley of the Culinary Classroom in Los Angeles, Nina Boski of LifeBites meditation and coaching, and herbalists Dr. Michael and Leslie Tierra of East West School of Planetary Herbology.

Deep appreciation goes out to my writing groups: The Merry Muses (Kimberly Nichols and Elizabeth Yochim) in Los Angeles and The Ladies Writing Society (Jocelyn "Jyoti" Kay Levy, Melissa Hrdinsky, and Tara Uziel) in San Francisco for their encouragement in helping me discover my voice and be steadfast in my purpose.

It's been amazing to have just about every chapter of my life represented in the actual making of this book. Many thanks to my childhood friend Travis Brown in Bluff Dale for his illustrations of everything from tea cup earth elements to lily pads. A heartfelt thank you to my University of Texas at Austin roommate Sheila Parr for the creation of the crisp ChakWave logo years ago, and now her beautiful book cover design and layout. A bow to Southern California based Kimberly Nichols for her thoughtful editing and to illustrator Steve Buccellato for bringing the Chakralyn comic character to life. Much gratitude to Bay Area Sadie Crofts for her bright illustrations of all the fruits, vegetables, herbs, and yoga bodies.

I thank my husband Todd for believing in me and giving me the time and space to organize these ideas. I am deeply grateful to experience life alongside him as my comforting, cosmic co-pilot. This book was mostly written during our dynamic daughters Uma Anaïs and Iris Eiletta's nap times and Wednesdays when their helpful grandparents Arlene and Steve Krieger hung out with them.

The girls keep breaking open my heart in previously unimaginable ways, and their health, happiness, and future were in the forefront of my mind as I wrote this guide. I typed up the manuscript with my very wise and purring sixteen year old feline friend Balka curled up between me and my laptop as she shared her calming energy. And finally, thank YOU for reading this book and putting the words into action.

ADVANCE PRAISE FOR CHAKWAVE

"With an original and innovative way to view fasting, *ChakWave* provides a new experience each day. Lovingly created for your cleansing and healing, it helps you get to the root of things—and to open every other chakra for that matter."
~Anodea Judith, PhD, author of *Wheels of Life* and *Eastern Body, Western Mind*

"At the end of the seven days, I felt so empowered I didn't want it to end. In fact, I spent three days easing back into solid foods. I was vibrant and connected. During the program, I was surprised to find that hunger and cravings were not an issue. I have a new level of oneness with my body. Giving it a rest from the business of digesting allowed it to communicate more clearly and set a new baseline of connection and partnership between body, mind, and spirit. I am permanently empowered."
~Zoë Kors

"ChakWave is a treasure! Not only are Jacquelyn's juices amazing and delicious, but she has a remarkable way of sharing her knowledge of the chakras where all can relate and are inspired to make a commitment to healthy living. I use her book to train my Wee Yogis teachers around the world."
~Jocelyn "Jyoti" Kay Levy

"ChakWave is a delicious blend of full, ripe taste, vibrant, stimulating color, sweet, sensual scents, and the perfect energetic boost for whatever you need that day!"
~Andrea Brook

"ChakWave is an amazingly comprehensive cleanse for the mind and body. The cleanse was expertly crafted by Jacquelyn, providing a thoughtful experience to nourish the physical and subtle bodies. All components were beautifully complementary, allowing for deep healing and rejuvenation. I felt renewed on many levels after I completed the program, and I can't wait for the next time!"
~Abby Yarger

"To see color in its full spectrum and vividness is a sign of health and a positive mood. ChakWave's juices bring attention to color as a reminder of the chakra system while providing nourishing support to the body on the inside. Health begins in the kitchen, and the more colorful the better!"
~Lina Augius, MD MPH

"ChakWave is more than a book on juicing, it's a blueprint for how to live an abundantly creative, nourished, and integrated life. Jacquelyn is intrepid in her appetite for research and innovation synthesizing this vibrantly conceived and communicated health and wellness plan. To live a ChakWave inspired life is to come home to a fully nourished self in mind, body and spirit."
~Elizabeth Yochim

"ChakWave is fantastic, refreshing, and nourishing. Being healthy should always taste this great! Love it. Viva ChakWave!"
~Norman Madrid

"For me, some juices tasted good, some juices made me giddy, while others felt like they were warming my soul."
~Lisa Delgin

"This is FANTASTIC!"
~Joshua Townshend

"While I try to eat healthy, I was always terrible at 'dieting' and never even went near doing a cleanse. But a friend talked me into doing the ChakWave juice cleanse . . . 'just try it for one day and you'll want to keep going,' she said. And she was totally right. I wasn't at all hungry or 'lacking' food, but I felt light and I had tons of energy. The juices are so yummy and filling. And by the 3rd day, my skin was noticeably glowing. And just as an extra plus, I was less bloated and lost a few pounds. Through the process, I learned a lot about my eating habits too. I have recommended this cleanse to so many people—I wish everyone could try it and experience these benefits!"
~Nikki Eisinger

"ChakWave is a spiritual, enlightening, yummy, healthy, great time!! I feel absolutely AMAZING!!"
~Andy Deal

"The extra love and attention that goes into this cosmic concoction of ChakWave juices does not go unnoticed by your mind, body, spirit or tastebuds! Each juice is a super-tasty-super-fusion, hand-crafted with its vibrant color and medicinal herbal properties formulated to align your corresponding chakras—like a magic mantra elixir!

Jacquelyn uses only the highest quality ingredients available with each juice "chak" full of only the freshest organic, fruits, veggies, herbs, seeds and superfoods! She is passionate, she's done her homework, and you'll taste it in every sip. I've used her juices and have followed her guide for seasonal detoxing on numerous occasions, and I come out vibrant, energized and glowing every time.

I've been a fresh juice-drinking vegan for years, having tried and tasted my share of various juice brands. I've found nothing on the market that comes close to ChakWave! If you're seeking your ideal juice or juice cleanse, look no further—ChakWave will have you refreshed, restored, rejuvenated and realigned!"
~Janette Gorney

"Wonderfully weird juices."
~Seth Godin

"I didn't have a juicer so used a blender to make the ChakWave recipes for my cleanse. I felt the effect upon the taste of my first glass. It's taught me how to feel my body, and now I know what it wants. Thank you Jacquelyn!"
~Joe P. Said

"I have a client who is struggling in her relationship so I sent her some of the info about the Root Chakra from your site, emphasizing the meditation and encouraging her to research the chakra on her own to re-ground herself. She just emailed me and is in a MUCH better place. Among other things, she bought herself a huge bouquet of red flowers and had her toenails painted red as a reminder. It made me smile—such a lovely image, and one inspired by ChakWave, so I wanted to share. Your impact is rippling out across the country."
~Catrina Gregory

"I'm so all about the green juice . . . blew me away in such a fine way. I've been thinking about it ever since."
~Erick Brownstein

"I discovered flavors while tasting ChakWave I never knew existed."
~Guru Thapar

"Losing weight was not my primary goal in doing your ChakWave cleanse. I truly just wanted to rid my body once and for all of the residual toxins built up in my system!

However, today, just for giggles as everything about me felt "lighter" I stepped on the scale . . . I AM DOWN 6 POUNDS!!!! It is the most weight I have lost since my recovery!!! I literally got off the scale, shook the scale, stepped back on to confirm my weight again and then started to cry!!! Until today, mentally I have felt like a much better version of my old self but physically I have had to stare at the damages caused from my year long battle with illness . . . that ended TODAY!!!"
~Alycia Herron

"ChakWave is a well thought out, clearly organized and profoundly powerful internal cleansing system that excites and ignites. Each day, you have things to look at in your life, pretty and tasty beverages, and body movements to integrate the whole powerhouse of chakra based body cleansing. Lucky you for finding this and the badass community connected to ChakWave."
~Geffen Rothe

"I had the privilege of cleansing with ChakWave and Jacquelyn for a full week last year just after the holidays. The love, energy, intention and knowledge she provided was life changing. The juices taste amazing and provide much more energy than my mind originally thought possible. I partook in the cleanse amidst a large career shift, and the clarity and calm ChakWave brought amidst that time was monumental. It allowed me to clearly listen, to be in touch with my true self and understand which decisions were best for my life not only in that moment but in the longterm. Since the cleanse, I've incorporated juicing into my life but now with the convenience of having her love sitting on my kitchen counter 365 days a year through this book will be incredible! If you are looking for mental, physical and spiritual clairvoyance and pure energy, ChakWave will definitely take you there! Thanks Jacquelyn."
~Seth Cotter

"Jacquelyn offers a very informative and easy-to-follow juice cleanse. She provides nutrient-dense juice recipes in every color of the rainbow. Just seven days is all that is needed to get real, practical, life-changing solutions to recharge and/or reclaim your health."
~Samantha Speck MS, RDN

"The ChakWave cleanse is like a total tune-up for the body, mind, and spirit. We do routine maintenance on cars and airplanes to ensure our survival—but what about ourselves? Fluent in a 5,000-year-old language, Jacquelyn facilitates healing by applying ancient chakra wisdom to our modern lives. Her juices provide a delicious foundation for an illumination—and they are only the beginning. The program produces longterm results by teaching you how to help yourself. Thanks to ChakWave, I have integrated new modalities into my wellness routine, and I feel more aligned and energetic than ever."
~Lucy Robinson

RESOURCES

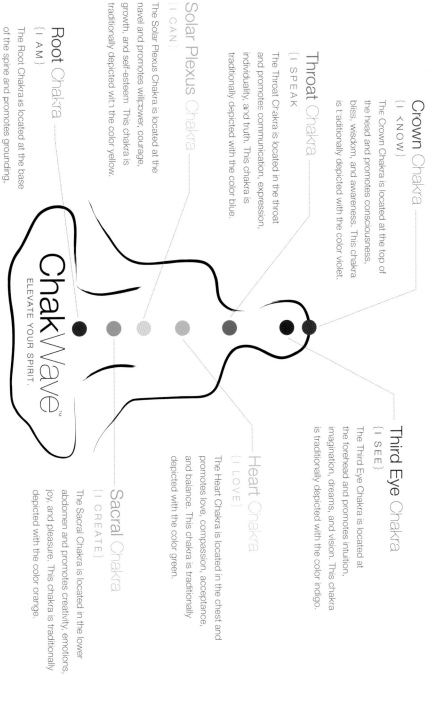

Crown Chakra
{ I < N O W }

The Crown Chakra is located at the top of the head and promotes consciousness, bliss, wisdom, and awareness. This chakra is traditionally depicted with the color violet.

Throat Chakra
{ I S P E A K }

The Throat Chakra is located in the throat and promotes communication, expression, individuality, and truth. This chakra is traditionally depicted with the color blue.

Solar Plexus Chakra
{ I C A N }

The Solar Plexus Chakra is located at the navel and promotes willpower, courage, growth, and self-esteem. This chakra is traditionally depicted with the color yellow.

Root Chakra
{ I A M }

The Root Chakra is located at the base of the spine and promotes grounding, security, prosperity, and trust. This chakra is traditionally depicted with the color red.

Third Eye Chakra
{ I S E E }

The Third Eye Chakra is located at the forehead and promotes intuition, imagination, dreams, and vision. This chakra is traditionally depicted with the color indigo.

Heart Chakra
{ I L O V E }

The Heart Chakra is located in the chest and promotes love, compassion, acceptance, and balance. This chakra is traditionally depicted with the color green.

Sacral Chakra
{ I C R E A T E }

The Sacral Chakra is located in the lower abdomen and promotes creativity, emotions, joy, and pleasure. This chakra is traditionally depicted with the color orange.

ChakWave™
ELEVATE YOUR SPIRIT.

Chakra Yoga Postures

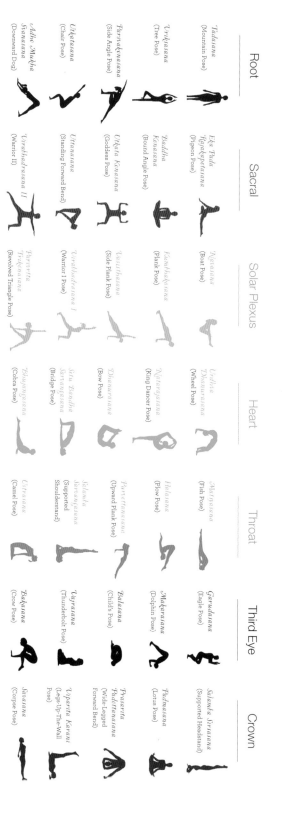

Root

Tadasana
(Mountain Pose)

Vrikasana
(Tree Pose)

Parsvakonasana
(Side Angle Pose)

Utkatasana
(Chair Pose)

Adho Mukha Svanasana
(Downward Dog)

Sacral

Eka Pada Rajakapotasana
(Pigeon Pose)

Baddha Konasana
(Bound Angle Pose)

Utkata Konasana
(Goddess Pose)

Uttanasana
(Standing Forward Bend)

Virabhadrasana II
(Warrior II)

Solar Plexus

Navasana
(Boat Pose)

Kumbhakasana
(Plank Pose)

Vasisthasana
(Side Plank Pose)

Virabhadrasana I
(Warrior I)

Parivrtta Trikonasana
(Revolved Triangle Pose)

Heart

Urdhva Dhanurasana
(Wheel Pose)

Natarajasana
(King Dancer Pose)

Dhanurasana
(Bow Pose)

Setu Bandha Sarvangasana
(Bridge Pose)

Bhujangasana
(Cobra Pose)

Throat

Matsyasana
(Fish Pose)

Halasana
(Plow Pose)

Purvottanasana
(Upward Plank Pose)

Salamba Sarvangasana
(Supported Shoulderstand)

Ustrasana
(Camel Pose)

Third Eye

Garudasana
(Eagle Pose)

Makarasana
(Dolphin Pose)

Balasana
(Child's Pose)

Vajrasana
(Thunderbolt Pose)

Bakasana
(Crow Pose)

Crown

Salamba Sirsasana
(Supported Headstand)

Padmasana
(Lotus Pose)

Prasarita Padottanasana
(Wide-Legged Forward Bend)

Viparita Karani
(Legs-Up-The-Wall Pose)

Savasana
(Corpse Pose)

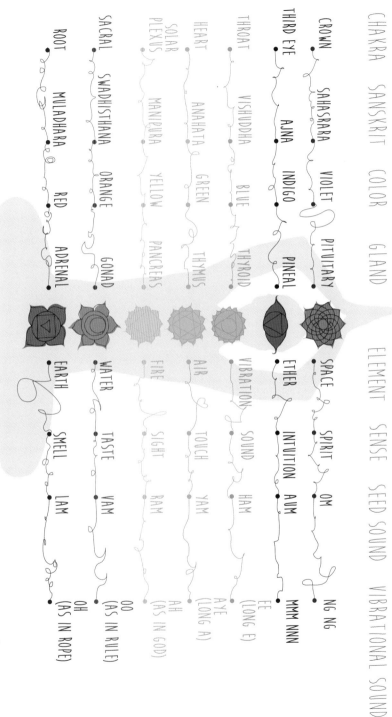

CHAKRA	SANSKRIT	COLOR	GLAND		ELEMENT	SENSE	SEED SOUND	VIBRATIONAL SOUND
CROWN	SAHASRARA	VIOLET	PITUITARY		SPACE	SPIRIT	OM	NG NG
THIRD EYE	AJNA	INDIGO	PINEAL		ETHER	INTUITION	AUM	MMM NNN
THROAT	VISHUDDHA	BLUE	THYROID		VIBRATION	SOUND	HAM	EE (LONG E)
HEART	ANAHATA	GREEN	THYMUS		AIR	TOUCH	YAM	AYE (LONG A)
SOLAR PLEXUS	MANIPURA	YELLOW	PANCREAS		FIRE	SIGHT	RAM	AH (AS IN GOD)
SACRAL	SWADHISTHANA	ORANGE	GONAD		WATER	TASTE	VAM	OO (AS IN RULE)
ROOT	MULADHARA	RED	ADRENAL		EARTH	SMELL	LAM	OH (AS IN ROPE)

CHAKWAVE

CHAKWAVE.COM